TRAVERSE
THEATRE

presents

THE ARCHITECT
by DAVID GREIG

First performance at the Traverse Theatre
Friday 23 February 1996

Subsequently at the Traverse Festival 1996
Tuesday 6 - Saturday 31 August

Originally commissioned by the Royal Court Theatre, London.

TRAVERSE THEATRE

Over the last three decades Edinburgh's Traverse Theatre has had a seminal influence on British and international theatre. With quality, award-winning productions and programming, the Traverse receives accolades at home and abroad from audiences and critics alike.

Traverse productions have been seen world-wide. After sell-out Edinburgh runs MOSCOW STATIONS transferred to both the West End and to New York, Off Broadway. UNIDENTIFIED HUMAN REMAINS AND THE TRUE NATURE OF LOVE and POOR SUPER MAN transferred to Hampstead Theatre, and after touring the Highlands and Islands of Scotland, KNIVES IN HENS transferred to a sell-out season at the Bush Theatre in London. This year BONDAGERS toured the world, delighting audiences in Edinburgh, London, Toronto and Budapest.

The Traverse is a power-house of quality experimentation, artistic diversity and the place to see some of the most important contemporary theatre work around. The Theatre commissions the best new writers from Scotland and around the world; facilitates numerous script development workshops, rehearsed readings and public writing workshops; and produces six major new theatre productions plus a Scottish touring production each year. An essential element of the Company's activities takes place within the educational sector, concentrating on the process of new writing in schools. The Traverse is unique in its exclusive dedication to new writing - providing the infrastructure, professional support and expertise to ensure the development of a sustainable and relevant theatre culture for Scotland.

For the 1996 Festival the Traverse Theatre Company presents David Greig's THE ARCHITECT, which returns to the Traverse stage following its tremendous success in the Spring. The Company also presents the world premiere of SHINING SOULS by Chris Hannan.

PLAYWRIGHT'S NOTE

I began wanting to write this play when I first encountered the phenomenon of the dying architects. A friend from Lanarkshire mentioned to me that the designer of Motherwell's town centre was supposed to have committed suicide when he saw his brutalist buildings complete. A friend in London told me the man who designed her tower block had jumped from the top of it in despair at its ugliness. The same thing had apparently happened in Haringey and Wester Hailes. In Germany, I was told about two different Stalinist architects who couldn't bear the sight of their works and preferred to die rather than see them again. Even the architect of Glasgow's Kelvingrove Museum jumped from one of the towers when he saw that his dream palace had been built back to front.

But the Kelvingrove in Glasgow wasn't built back to front and in my researches I could come up with no recorded cases of architects taking their own lives in these circumstances. In fact they seemed quite pleased with even their most unpopular works. The architect death stories are urban myths. What drew me to the stories was the feeling that the inhabitants of these tower blocks and housing estates wanted the stories to be true. They wanted punishment. Communities seemed to be taking collective psychic revenge on the designers of the environment.

That summer saw the demolition of Basil Spence's Queen's Court building in Glasgow. The crowd was huge, many more than police expected. It was a glorious hot day, people took time off work, the whole city was interested. The event was covered live on television and local radio. The demolition had more of the atmosphere of a public execution than of urban renewal. I was curious about this urge to watch structure fall and I was reminded of my own childhood ambition of pushing a detonator plunger slowly down and watching a skyscraper crumple into rubble.

THE ARCHITECT came out of a long process of writing. Writing about families, writing about cities and writing about politics. It has been through a number of drafts and a number of stories but, at heart, I think it's just a response to my own feelings about the collapse of tall buildings.

David Greig
1996

THE ARCHITECT

Leo Black	**Alexander Morton**
Martin Black	**Tom Smith**
Sheena Mackie	**Una McLean**
Paulina Black	**Morag Hood**
Dorothy Black	**Ashley Jensen**
Joe	**John Stahl**
Billy	**Paul Hickey**

Director	**Philip Howard**
Designer	**Simon Vincenzi**
Lighting Designer	**Chahine Yavroyan**
Composer	**Reuben Taylor**
Assistant Director	**John Tiffany**
Stage Manager	**Gavin Johnston**
Deputy Stage Manager	**Kay Courteney-Chrystal**
Assistant Stage Manager	**Victoria Paulo**
Wardrobe Supervisor	**Lynn Ferguson**
Wardrobe Assistant	**Alice Taylor**

DAVID GREIG: Theatre work includes: EUROPE (Traverse, Deutsches Theater - Berlin, Staatstheater - Chemnitz). David co-founded Suspect Culture with Graham Eatough which has produced - AIRPORT (Traverse/Tramway Commission); A SAVAGE REMINISCENCE (Edinburgh Fringe, nominated for Guardian Student Drama Award), AND THE OPERA HOUSE REMAINED UNBUILT, AN AUDIENCE WITH SATAN, THE GARDEN, STALINLAND (Edinburgh Fringe First Winner), CONSIDER THE DISH, PETRA'S EXPLANATION, STATIONS ON THE BORDER and ONE WAY STREET (Traverse and German tour in late November). David's film debut, NIGHTLIFE, was premiered at the Drambuie Edinburgh Film Festival in 1995 and will be shown on BBC2 later this year. David is currently under commission to the Traverse and the National Theatre Studio. He was recently awarded a Thames Television Theatre Writer's Bursary to work with the RSC.

PAUL HICKEY (Billy): Trained: RSAMD. Theatre work includes: SAILMAKER, TWELFTH NIGHT (TAG); A NIGHT OF GENTLE SEX COMEDIES (Theatre Positive Scotland); ONE FLEW OVER THE CUCKOO'S NEST, MACBETH, STILL LIFE, ECSTASY, WASTED (Raindog); MERLIN THE MAGNIFICENT AND THE ADVENTURES OF ARTHUR (Cumbernauld); JUMP THE LIFE TO COME (7:84); THE SLAB BOYS, CUTTIN' A RUG (Young Vic). TV work includes: TAGGART, HIGH ROAD, THE BRIT OIL FRAUD (STV); THE SWEETEST FEELING (Starcatch). Radio work includes: BATTLE OF THE AIRWAVES, BODIES OCCUPATION, THE BASEMENT TAPES, SCOTTISH RESOURCES, ROCK & ROLL PEARLS (BBC). Film work includes: NIGHTLIFE (BBC); CHARMED (Edinburgh Video Training); CAFE RENDEVOUS, WANTING AND GETTING.

MORAG HOOD (*Paulina*): Theatre work includes: THE MASTER BUILDER (Royal Lyceum/Riverside Studios); THE BIG PICNIC (The Shed, Glasgow); IL CAMPIELLO, VOLPONE, THE LADY FROM MAXIMS, THE HUNCHBACK OF NOTRE DAME, BOW DOWN, LARKRISE TO CANDLEFORD, THE ICEMAN COMETH (National); A STREETCAR NAMED DESIRE (Piccadilly); THE TRAVELLER (Almeida); THEN AND NOW, A LITTLE LIKE DROWNING (Hampstead); I LOVE MY LOVE (Orange Tree); MARRAKECH (Lyric Studio); HOLIDAYS (West Yorkshire Playhouse); HAMLET (Belgrade); SINGING OUTSIDE HEAVEN (Chamber Group of Scotland); PETER PAN (Yorkshire Playhouse). TV work includes: THE GOVENOR II, THE BIG PICNIC, WAR AND PEACE, HARRY, THE CAMERONS, JANE EYRE, BERGERAC, SENSE OF GUILT, IPHIGENIA AT AULIS, TELL TALE HEART (BBC); BREEZE ANSTEY, PERSUASION, FAMILIES (Granada); AUF WIEDERSEHEN PET (Central); A TASTE FOR DEATH (Anglia); BERLIN BREAKS (Oceanic Film Productions).

PHILIP HOWARD (*Director*): Trained: Royal Court Theatre on the Regional Theatre Young Director Scheme. For the Traverse: LOOSE ENDS, BROTHERS OF THUNDER, GRACE IN AMERICA, EUROPE, MARISOL, KNIVES IN HENS (also Bush Theatre), THE ARCHITECT, FAITH HEALER. For the Royal Court Young People's Theatre: THROWING STONES and the 1991 YOUNG WRITERS' FESTIVAL. Other theatre includes: HIPPOLYTUS (Arts, Cambridge); ENTERTAINING MR SLOANE (Royal, Northampton); SOMETHING ABOUT US (Lyric Hammersmith Studio). Philip was a director at Dràma Nàiseanta na h-Oigridh on the Isle of Benbecula from its foundation in 1989 until 1992 and has been Associate Director at the Traverse since 1993. He takes up the post of Artistic Director of the Traverse in October of this year.

ASHLEY JENSEN (*Dorothy*): Trained: Queen Margaret College. Theatre work includes: UGANDA (Royal Court Upstairs and National Theatre Studio); THE BIG PICNIC (Harland & Wolff Shed); THE PRIME OF MISS JEAN BRODIE (Royal Lyceum); THE GUID SISTERS, THE REAL WURLD?, THE TREASURE OF WOOKIMAGOO, SALVATION (Tron); RAB C. NESBITT (BBC Comedy); CARLUCCIO AND THE QUEEN OF HEARTS (Fifth Estate and Hampstead); THE SNOW QUEEN, THE CRUCIBLE (Citizens); THE RESISTIBLE RISE OF ARTURO UI (7:84); 'OOR WILLIE (Jimmy Logan's Co); MANDY REDMAYNE STEPS INTO A STORY (Pocket, Cumbria). TV work includes: BAD BOYS, TAKING OVER THE ASYLUM, PARAHANDY, DOWN AMONG THE BIG BOYS, RAB C. NESBITT, DREAMING, BAD BOYS (BBC); CAPITAL LIVES - TEMP, MAY TO DECEMBER (Cinema Verity); ROUGHNECKS (First Choice); THE BILL (ITV); TICKETS FOR THE ZOO (Cormorant Films).

UNA McLEAN (*Sheena*): Theatre work includes: SKY WOMAN FALLING, INES DE CASTRO, BLENDING IN (Traverse); BEGGAR'S OPERA, FIDDLER ON THE ROOF (Scottish Opera); REVOLTING PEASANTS (7:84); CINDERELLA (The King's); THE STEAMIE (National Tour); BOURGEOIS GENTILHOMME (Dundee Rep); THE GUID SISTERS, PADDY'S MARKET (The Tron); WOMEN IN MIND, ARSENIC & OLD LACE, THE LITTLE FOXES (Pitlochry Festival Theatre); ANNIE (Perth Rep). TV work includes: BETWEEN THE LINES, CITY LIGHTS, DREAMING (BBC); DID YOU SEE UNA?, CAPTAIN BONNY.

ALEXANDER MORTON (*Leo*): Theatre work includes: SLAB BOYS TRILOGY (Traverse); ONE FLEW OVER THE CUCKOO'S NEST, MACBETH (Raindog); NO MEAN CITY, THE SASH (7:84); ROBERT BURNS (Scottish Theatre Co); UNCLE VANYA (Royal Lyceum); THE MAIDEN STONE (Hampstead); AN EXPERIENCED WOMAN GIVES ADVICE (Royal Exchange, Manchester). TV work includes: WAITING FOR ELVIS, EXTRAS, TAGGART (STV); BETWEEN THE LINES (BBC); FIRM FRIENDS I & II (Zenith / Tyne Tees); THE ONE THAT GOT AWAY (LWT); BAD BOYS, LOVE ME TENDER (BBC). Radio work includes: TUNES OF GLORY, DOCTOR JEKYLL AND MR HYDE (BBC).

TOM SMITH (*Martin*): Trained: RSAMD. Theatre work includes: BROTHERS OF THUNDER (Traverse); UNIDENTIFIED HUMAN REMAINS AND THE TRUE NATURE OF LOVE (Traverse/Hampstead); HENRY VI PART III (RSC World Tour); LANARK (TAG/Edinburgh International Festival); GOOD (Tron/Edinburgh International Festival). Television work includes: TICKETS FOR THE ZOO, MY DEAD DAD (C4); TAGGART, THE BILL (ITV); CARDIAC ARREST, RAB C NESBITT, 2000 NOT OUT (BBC). Film work includes: TROUBLE (Bluestone Pictures). Radio work includes: THE LIFE CLASS, RUNNING BEFORE THE WIND, WAVERLEY, DR JEKYLL AND MR HYDE, THE SERPENT'S BACK, TUNES OF GLORY (BBC).

JOHN STAHL (*Joe*): Trained RSAMD. Theatre work includes: THE BATTLE OF BAREFOOT (Theatre Space); NEXT TIME I'LL SING TO YOU, THE GAME (Edinburgh Festival); ALADDIN, THE CARETAKER, WHAT THE BUTLER SAW, THE GLASS MENAGERIE, ZOO STORY, ENTERTAINING MR SLOANE (Cumbernauld); THE SASH AND THE GAME (Glasgow Pavilion); LENT (Lyric); COMMEDIA (Sheffield Crucible/Lyric/King's, Edinburgh); MACBETH, THE SLEEPING BEAUTY, PADDY'S MARKET, THE REAL WURLD? (Tron); DEATH OF A SALESMAN, THE SNOW QUEEN, THE CRUCIBLE (Lyceum); ALADDIN (Adam Smith); HAMLET, COMEDIANS (Belgrade, Coventry); CINDERELLA (Dundee Rep). Television includes: YOU'RE A GOOD BOY, SON, A SENSE OF FREEDOM, GARNOCK WAY, HIGH ROAD, ALBERT AND THE LION, CRIME STORY, TAGGART (STV); THE McKINNONS, RESORT TO MURDER, PARAHANDY, DR FINLAY (BBC). Film work includes LOCH NESS.

REUBEN TAYLOR (*Composer*): Trained: RSAMD. Theatre work includes: THE OWL AND THE PUSSYCAT (Edinburgh Graduate Theatre); FLOWERS IN THEIR HAIR (Tweed Theatre). Film work includes: PRIEST ISLAND, THE KEEPER (Edinburgh Film Festival). Reuben has also worked extensively as a keyboard player with live bands HOT SAUSAGE and THE BLAZE FAKERS.

JOHN TIFFANY (*Assistant Director*): Trained: Glasgow University. Assistant Director at the Traverse since August 1995. He has directed SHARP SHORTS and co-directed STONES AND ASHES for the Traverse. Other work includes: THE SUNSET SHIP (Young Vic); GRIMM TALES (Leicester Haymarket). Whilst at University John set up LOOKOUT, a new writing theatre company, for whom his directing work includes HIDE AND SEEK, BABY and EAT UP which he co-wrote with Vicky Featherstone. He has also worked as a script editor for Ikona Films.

SIMON VINCENZI (*Designer*): Theatre work includes: TOURIST VARIATIONS/ANNA (Traverse); THE SLEEP (Mayfest); MADE WITH UNREASON (Tramway); THREEPENNY OPERA (Scottish Opera); 15 MINUTES TO 6 HOURS (Anatomy Dance Theatre); THE CARRIER FREQUENCY (Impact Theatre Co-op); GERMINAL (Paines Plough); THE CHERRY ORCHARD (Sheffield Crucible); THERESE RAQUIN (Nottingham Playhouse); BABY DOLL (National); TEOREMA (International Tour). With Rose English directing he designed WALKS ON WATER (Hackney Empire); THE DOUBLE WEDDING, TANTAMOUNT ESPERANCE (Royal Court). Simon directed HEARTLESS (ICA), choreographed and designed ONCE UPON AND EVER AFTER (Purcell Room) and is associate director for Towering Inferno's concert KADDISH. Future projects include two video installations, BLACK and THE DISAPPEARANCE.

CHAHINE YAVROYAN (*Lighting Designer*): Trained: Bristol Old Vic School. Theatre work includes: THE TRIAL, METAMORPHOSIS, MISS JULIE, ZOO STORY, AGAMEMNON (London Theatre Group); PEOPLE SHOWS NO.84 - NO.101 (People Show); MACBETH (Leicester Haymarket); USES OF ENCHANTMENT (ICA); THE LITTLE BLACK BOOK (The French Institute); GLORIA, I SURRENDER DEAR (The Place); HAUGHMOND DANCES (Haughmond Abbey); ASCENDING FIELDS (Fort Dunlop); ENNIO MARCHETTO (Hackney Empire); LA MUSICA DEUXIEMME, GAUCHO (Hampstead); HEDDA GABLER (Manchester Royal Exchange); HOUSE (Site Specific show in Salisbury); PYGMALION (Nottingham Playhouse); DARWIN'S FLOOD (Bush); 15 MINUTES TO 6 HOURS (Anatomy Dance Theatre); TANTAMOUNT ESPERANCE (Royal Court).

TRAVERSE THEATRE
THE COMPANY

TRAVERSE THEATRE

SPONSORSHIP

Sponsorship income enables the Traverse to commission and produce new plays and offer audiences a diverse and exciting programme of events throughout the year.

We would like to thank the following companies for their support throughout the year.

BANK OF SCOTLAND
A FRIEND FOR LIFE

ESPC
working together with the TRAVERSE THEATRE

CORPORATE ASSOCIATE SCHEME

LEVEL ONE
Clydesdale Bank
Dundas & Wilson CS
Scottish Brewers
Scottish Equitable plc
Scottish Life Assurance Co
United Distillers

LEVEL TWO
Allingham & Co, Solicitors
Isle of Skye 8 Year Blend
NB Information
Mactaggart and Mickel Ltd
The Royal Bank of Scotland
Willis Corroon Scotland Ltd
Métier Recruitment

LEVEL THREE
Alistir Tait FGA Antique & Fine Jewellery, Gerrard & Medd Designers, KPMG, Scottish Post Office Board, Nicholas Groves Raines Architects, Moores Rowland Chartered Accountants

With thanks to Navy Blue Design, designers for the Traverse and to George Stewarts the printers.

The Traverse Theatre's work would not be possible without the support of:

·EDINBVRGH·
THE CITY OF EDINBURGH COUNCIL

THE SCOTTISH ARTS COUNCIL

The Traverse receives financial assistance for its educational and development work from: Calouste Gulbenkian Foundation, Esmee Fairbairn Charitable Trust, The Peggy Ramsay Foundation, The Nancie Massey Charitable Trust

THE ARCHITECT props, costumes & scenery built by Traverse workshops.

Funded by the National Lottery

THE SCOTTISH ARTS COUNCIL

National Lottery Fund

Print Photography by Euan Myles. Production Photography by Sean Hudson
LEVER BROTHERS for Wardrobe Care

Registered Charity No. SCO 02368

For Mum, Dad and Mike

No Matter. Try Again.
Fail Again. Fail Better.

Samuel Beckett

'The Smoke'

A little house among trees by the lake
From the roof smoke rises
Without it
How dreary would be
House, trees and lake.

Bertolt Brecht

Characters

Leo Black, *an architect, fifties.*
Paulina Black, *his wife, forties.*
Martin Black, *his son, twenties.*
Dorothy Black, *his daughter, twenties.*
Joe, *a lorry driver, forties.*
Billy, *a young man, twenties.*
Sheena Mackie, *a campaigner, fifties.*

Setting: A city. The present.

I would like to thank the following people and institutions who have helped in the production of this, and earlier drafts of *The Architect* . . .

The Traverse Theatre, the cast of the Royal Court *Architect* workshop, Mel Kenyon, Graham Eatough, Callum Cuthbertson, Jill Riddiford, Catherine Lindow, Melvyn Greig, Mike Cullen, David Harrower, Harriet Braun and Lucie Macaulay whose phlegmy coughs were always welcome.

Act One

1

Darkness.
The long blast of a siren.
A moment of silence.
A series of explosions.
Large buildings falling to the ground.
A crowd applauding.

2

A summer afternoon.
A building site.

A small trestle table stands centre stage. On the table are architectural plans and blueprints. The papers are weighted down with stones to stop them blowing away. Two hard hats are on the table.

Martin *is looking casually at the blueprints.*
Leo *enters carrying an architectural model, it is bulky, he is struggling with it.* **Martin** *looks.*

Leo   Some professions, Martin, exist only or mainly, to provide particular people with a congenial way of earning their living. Publishing, for example, or radio, you mentioned radio. These people, these publishers and so on, they're interesting. I've met them sometimes. They're creative people. Their surroundings are, if you like, seductive. But in the end, these are people without effect in the world. Do you see what I'm saying. They have no . . . power to shape, no responsibility. Now, building, construction, engineering, architecture . . . these have effects. Here you have responsibility. Obviously you can dream, use your imagination, of course, but there's a purpose . . . you put your dreams on paper . . . blueprints, drawings.

Your smallest line, the merest gesture of the pencil, can be the curve of a motorway flyover, or pull a tower up from the slums, or shape a square from a mess of alleys. That's what we do, Martin, we dream these structures and then . . .

Martin   It's flat.

Leo   Sorry?

Martin   This. Here. I thought you built. I thought you were a builder. This is flat.

Leo   This is the car park. It's supposed to be flat.

Martin   Oh.

Leo   To go back, we dream these structures, these buildings and . . .

Martin   You said there was going to be a tower. There's a tower on the model.

Leo   . . . the buildings take shape, become solid . . .

Martin   There's no tower here.

Leo   . . . people live in them, work in them . . .

Martin   There's some lumps.

Leo   We have an effect. You understand?

Martin *refers to the model.*

Martin   Nothing like that.

Leo   The tower's going to be over there. At the head of the docks. Where the fish market used to be. They're still digging foundations. But you can imagine . . .

Martin   Is this one of yours? The tower? Did you dream it?

Leo   A lot of people are involved on the project.

Martin   Did you think it up though? Your dream?

Leo   I'm part of the design team, obviously . . . so in that sense, yes. Everyone has their role, everyone has input.

Martin   What's your input?

Leo Well, the car park's mine . . . my job on the team is access. So clearly . . . parking . . . which is important on a project like this . . . also security . . . the walls, if you like.

Martin They're big.

Leo Well spotted.

Martin Thick.

Leo Look around you, Martin . . . beyond the fencing, over there . . . what do you see?

Martin Houses. Some people.

Leo Houses, yes, but . . . look at the immediate environment . . . the surroundings . . .

Martin . . .

Leo Understand? This site's in the middle of no-man's-land. Look at it. Devastation. Someone in the planning department told me, this is officially third world status. Which means vandalism, burglars, and Christ knows whatever else. It's a prime example . . .
You dream up ideas, but you have to think, you have to see potential problems. Solve them. Before they happen . . . understand? . . . I saw the problem . . . that . . . and this is the physical solution.

Martin Big walls.

Leo Metaphorically, yes, I suppose so.

Martin How high?

Leo Four metres, plus barbed wire . . .

Martin The tower. How high?

Leo Square footage?

Martin How many floors?

Leo Seventeen.

Martin How high can you build something?

Leo In what way do you mean high?

Martin   Up the way high? How high can a thing be built? Anything?

Leo   It's an interesting question.

Martin   Interesting.

Leo   Design, materials and nature are what you have to think about. A good design can take poor materials higher. Good materials can support a poor design. And then there's nature – wind, damp, heat, earthquakes . . . the imponderables . . . you overcompensate for nature . . .

Martin   How high then?

Leo   The base of the building would have to be wide . . . to support the height. Lifts are a problem, over a certain number of floors and you need separate lifts . . . then there's the human elements . . . vertigo. People do get vertigo. I suppose that counts as nature. Materials, design and nature . . . if one of these factors is out of harmony then, when you get beyond a certain point, the structure overbalances, things get dangerous. You can work it out. Theoretically, though, there's no limits.

Martin   Can you build a thing high enough that if you fell off you wouldn't hit the ground?

Leo   . . .

Martin   High enough so that if you fell, you'd fall into orbit?

Leo   This is offices, Martin. No one's going to fall out.

Martin   Could you though?

Leo   Is this a joke?

Martin   I'm only asking how . . .

Leo   It feels like you're making a joke.

Martin   I'm not, honestly.

Leo   I thought you wanted to talk about work.

Martin   I was.

Leo   If you're bored . . .

Martin   I'm not bored . . . I was asking a question.

Leo   It sounded like a joke. I'm sorry. I didn't . . .

Martin   Doesn't matter. Forget it.

Leo   Put this on.

Leo *gives* **Martin** *a hard hat.*

Martin   What for?

Leo   Safety. It's to protect your head.

Martin   From what?

Leo   Everyone on site has to wear a hard hat. It's regulations.

Martin   But there's nothing above us. It's flat. Only lumps.

Leo   We're on site, Martin. Accidents happen. You'll wear a hard hat.

Martin   I'm just saying . . .

Leo   What the hell is the problem with you?
There's no pain in wearing it.
It won't hurt your head.
I said to put it on.

Martin *puts the hat on.*

Martin   I look like one of the Village People.

Leo   What?

Martin   Doesn't matter.

Leo   You mutter, Martin, do you know that? You're a mutterer. Under your breath. You speak behind your hand. Do you notice yourself doing it?

Martin (*muttering*)   No.

Leo   If you've got something to say. Say it clearly.
Make the point.
. . .
You have to think about your presentation.

Think about how you come across.

. . .

He offers **Martin** *a cigarette.*

Martin   I don't smoke.

Leo   Quite right too.

He tries to light his cigarette. He can't get the lighter to work.

Too windy.

He turns and cups his hand. The lighter still doesn't work.

Damn.

He lifts his jacket to use as a windbreak. Again he fails.

Damn.

Martin   I thought you'd given up.

Leo   Not yet.

Martin   Mum said she didn't let you smoke in the house any more.

Leo   We're not in the house.

Martin   Die if you want to.

Leo   You're muttering again. Stand here.

Martin *stands in front of* **Leo** *to block the wind.*

Martin   I said, 'Die if you want to.'

Leo   Closer.

Martin *stands closer.*

Martin   Man your age. Your job. You're probably due a stroke.

Leo   Closer.

Martin *and* **Leo** *stand uncomfortably close. The cigarette is finally lit.* **Martin** *moves away.*

Leo   So. What do you think?

Martin   About what?

Leo   The work. Does it appeal?

Martin   . . . ?

Leo   Are you interested or not?

Martin   . . . ?

Leo   Do you want the job?

Martin   What job?

Leo   What do you think I've been talking about?

Martin   I don't know. Stuff.

Leo   I wanted you to see the work.
I'm offering you a job, Martin.
You don't do anything . . . you're drifting . . . you don't . . .
I've been thinking, for a while now, just the time hasn't been
right, I've been considering the idea of setting up on my own.
Small scale. Nothing big, not yet anyway. It's only an idea at
the moment but this job's coming to an end and . . .
I want to get back to . . .
a certain control . . . understand?
This work, there's prestige but there's no control.

Martin   Who builds the models?

Leo   Never mind the model. Are you interested?

Martin   You used to let me play with these, when you'd
finished with them. I put toy soldiers in the buildings . . . I
staged riots, assassinations and things, street to street
fighting, car bombs and earthquakes . . .

Leo   They're technical models. They're not toys.

Martin   They're so delicate. So perfect. They look solid
but you only have to nudge them and something breaks.

Leo   You could have damaged them.

Martin   The model's clean . . . Is that deliberate? When
you make them? They don't look anything like real
buildings. There's no dirt. No mess around them. Just white
card, patches of green felt and pretend trees. They look like

film buildings. They look as though the sun's always shining on them.

Leo   Do you want to work with me or not?

. . .

It would be a job.

Martin   Can I do the models?

Leo   You'd have to start at the bottom . . . but you'd be trained. I could start you off with . . .

Martin   I could be in charge of making the models look real. Cover the walls in graffiti or something . . . put little models of dossers under the bridges . . . Use my know-how . . . Could I do that?

Leo   Why don't we have a look at the foundations?

Martin   Whatever you say, boss . . .

Leo   You can see how the building takes shape.

Martin   Whatever you want, boss.

Sheena *has entered. She stands by the model. She is carrying some papers.*

Leo   I want to know what you want, Martin. I know what I want. I'm trying to help you.

Martin   Dad, there's . . .

Leo   I don't expect you to be interested, you know. You don't have to pretend . . . Obviously you're interested in other things. Whatever. I don't know. You don't tell me. If you told me, maybe I could get in touch with someone . . .

Martin   Foundations . . . fine. Dad . . . there's a woman . . .

Leo   You mentioned radio. Maybe I could ring someone . . .

Martin   Cheers. But . . .

Leo   I have some contacts. I just thought it was possible you'd be interested in working for me.

Martin   I said. I said I was interested.

Leo Don't do me any favours.

Martin All right. I'm not interested.

Leo Well, what then? What exactly do you want?

Martin ...
Do you need a bicycle courier?

Sheena Excuse me.

Leo Sorry?

Martin I tried to tell you.

Sheena Mr Black?

Martin She's been stood there waiting.

Sheena Leo Black? Sorry to bother you. My name's Sheena Mackie. I haven't caught you at a bad time, have I?

Leo No ... I'm sorry. Are you supposed to be here?

Sheena I'll only take a minute. I've got a taxi waiting.

Leo Do you have a site pass?

Sheena I didn't know I needed one?

Leo No one's allowed on site without a pass ... I'm sorry it's regulations ...

Sheena Well. I'm here now so ... maybe we could have a chat ...

Leo It's Saturday morning, Mrs ...

Sheena Mackie, it's actually Ms. As I say, I'll only be a minute, the thing is I've tried to get you at your office, but you always seem to be busy ... I don't know if you remember the letter? I've put a copy in with the petition.

Leo Petition? You've lost me.

Sheena I'm the tenants' representative. From Eden Court.
We wrote to you about the flats weeks ago now.

Leo   What letter?
I haven't seen any . . .
Just a minute. Martin, could you get the phone from the car?

Sheena   I wouldn't normally bother you but things are
moving on. We need to keep things going. For the campaign.
Your wife said you'd be down here. I thought I'd take the
chance to catch you.

Leo   There's obviously been some . . .
Some kind of mix up.
I'm sure we can sort it out. The thing is . . . you need a site
pass. You understand we can't have people wandering
round, in case there's an accident. If you hold on, my son'll
ring the security people. Martin, could you give Mrs Mackie
your hat. While you're on site you need a hard hat. In case
anything falls on your head. For insurance . . .

Martin *gives her his hat.*

Leo *begins reading the folder of papers.*

Sheena   I feel like the Queen visiting the shipyards.

Martin   What about me?

Leo   What?

Martin   I don't have a hat now.

Leo   Just get the phone.

Sheena   I won't be a minute. The meter's running. Is that
your son?

Martin   Do you want me to answer?

Leo   He helps me.

Sheena   Are you a builder as well?

Leo   Architect.

Martin   Bicycle courier.

Sheena   Well. Pleased to meet you . . .

Martin   Martin.
Do you still want me to get the phone?

Leo Yes.

Sheena Like Dean Martin.

Martin What?

Sheena Before your time.

Martin No.

Leo I don't follow this, Mrs Mackie.
This petition you've got here.
This correspondence.
It's been sorted out. The council have spoken to me about the
Eden Court flats. I've talked to them about it. They're going
to refurbish them . . . I've sent designs . . . I don't see what
you're getting at.

Martin Martin Sheen maybe.

Sheena You didn't know?

Leo No.

Sheena I'm not sure how to say this.
The problem is . . . we . . .
I mean, us, the tenants . . . we don't want the flats
refurbished.

Martin Martin Luther King.

Bored, **Martin** *has begun to play with the model* [*piling buildings on
top of each other*] *Moving them around.*

Leo But they need work. Some of those blocks haven't been
maintained for years . . .

Martin Martina Navratilova.

Leo I told the housing executive. They'll fall apart if work
isn't done on them soon. The surveyor's report was . . .
Martin, don't do that!

Martin Just curious.

Leo The problem's under control. The work's being done
for you.

Sheena   We don't want the flats done up, Mr Black. We want them knocked down.

Leo   . . .

Sheena   We've got a petition. Signed by every resident. That copy's for you. There's a copy gone to the council, one to the paper and one to Prince Charles. He signed it.

Leo   Christ.

Sheena   Well, he's interested in that sort of thing, isn't he? Buildings. He's concerned. Not professionally but like an ordinary person. Isn't he?

Leo   He's not an architect. No.

Sheena   Mr Black, we just want houses. We've been in Eden Court, some of us, for twenty years . . .
This isn't a new problem. We've tried but things have gone too far now. We're not interested in plastering over the cracks any more. We want to live in proper houses, decently built.

Leo   I see.

Sheena   It's nothing personal.

Leo   Of course.

Sheena   No offence.

Leo   None taken.

Sheena   You'll consider the petition then?

Leo   I don't really see how I can help you.

Sheena   You can give us your support.

Leo   To demolish my own buildings?

Sheena   Our flats.

Leo   My design.

Martin   You could bomb them.

Leo   I don't see why you need my signature.
I'd have thought there was plenty people who wanted to see
the back of Eden Court.

Martin   From the sky. Planes.

Leo   People in this country don't like anything unless it's
thatched.

Martin   Smart bombs.

Sheena   The council don't want to build a new estate.
They say there isn't the money. It's cheaper to slap a bit of
paint on and leave the place to fall apart. We could take
them to court but something like this could take years. The
only way we'll get what we want is if we embarrass the
council. And if you say they need to be rebuilt they'll have to
do something. They can hardly argue with the architect, can
they?

Leo   Or Prince Charles.
. . .
You're very well organised, Mrs Mackie. This is . . . it's
impressive.

Sheena   Thank you.

Leo   You've put a lot of work into it.

Sheena   We have.

Leo   There's obviously . . . a lot of strong feeling in what
you say.

Sheena   Obviously.

Leo   But the feelings are misdirected, I'm afraid.
The Eden Court flats are good buildings.
Technically.

Martin   What's wrong with them.

Sheena   They're cold, the lifts don't work . . .

Leo   [There's nothing wrong with the design.]

Martin   Is that all?

Sheena   Most of the flats are infested with cockroaches.

Leo   There wasn't enough money spent on them at the time ...

Martin   Get Rentokil.

Leo   But if the council are prepared to spend the money now I don't see the need for destruction.

Sheena   They're a new breed of cockroach. A new mutation. There's been a documentary.

Leo   If you look at my proposals ...

Sheena   They can't be killed in the ordinary way.

Leo   I realise that, I understand there's a depth of emotion. Tower blocks do cause ... passion. I know that. But if I could ... persuade you about this ... I don't think there needs to be ...

Sheena   We're not asking you to say sorry or anything, Mr Black. We just want you to consider the petition. These signatures. That's the people that live in Eden Court ...

Leo   But destruction ...

Sheena   People get things wrong ... that's fair enough.

Leo   These are understandable grievances but ...

Sheena   You've got a chance to help fix it.

Leo   Individual problems like this can be solved.

Sheena   You've got a chance to make things right.

Leo   You can't just blow something up for no reason ... You can't just destroy something that's perfectly sound ...

Sheena   Look, Mr Black. The taxi's waiting. Now that we've met. Actually made contact. Maybe I could arrange an appointment. Talk to you once you've read everything.

Leo   I won't change my mind. I'm sorry.

Sheena   You know, it's funny to think it was you that built them.

Leo Is it?

Sheena Not you in particular. I just mean it's funny to think someone thought them up. You know, a person. You always feel as though they just happened. You're not insulted, are you?

Leo I assure you . . .

Sheena It's just . . . seeing you. Face to face, I mean. It's funny.
Well. I'll be in touch. (*To* **Martin**.) Nice to have met you.

Sheena *leaves.* **Martin** *considers the model. Now considerably rearranged.*

Leo Jesus Christ.

Martin Boom.

Leo What?

Martin Boom.

Lights down.

3

Later. A suburban garden. **Dorothy** *is sitting on a deckchair wearing a short summer dress and sunglasses. A radio is playing quietly beside her. On a table in the garden is a pile of delicate sandwiches and a jug of lemonade.* **Paulina** *is examining her plants. She is overdressed for the sun and wearing gardening gloves. She touches a plant.*

Paulina Black. See? Half an inch of black poison on the stem. You should cover up. That's just what's hanging in the air. It's worse in the sunshine. Some sort of chemical reaction takes place with the sun, makes it worse, apparently. You should cover up. You'll burn. If that's what's hanging in the air, imagine what's settling in your lungs and blood and everything. Illnesses are up. Cancers are up. Sicknesses are up. Dorothy? Are you listening to me. You'll burn alive under that sun. Dorothy?

She smells a rose.

No scent. Proof. If proof were needed. The scent's been poisoned out of them. They only look like flowers now. You have to ask yourself what next. I saw a cyclist stop at the lights. Imagine cycling, in this city, you could be dragged off and beaten at any junction. He was wearing a surgeon's mask. It was black. The gauze was black as tar. Like a swab soaked in black blood. That's just what's in the air.

An aeroplane passes loudly overhead.

Dorothy.
Dorothy.
Dorothy!

The noise has quietened. The radio still plays.

You should cover up. You should cover up before whatever's going to fall from the sky falls from the sky and gets on to your skin. Your father'll be back soon.

. . .

She makes her way indoors.

. . . You won't tan, you know. You don't tan. You'll burn. Look like a bad tomato. You should put some proper clothes on.

Paulina *exits. The radio continues to play.* **Dorothy** *hitches her skirt up her legs a little and rubs oil into them. She relaxes back in the deckchair. After some moments* **Leo** *enters. He is hot. He walks in front of* **Dorothy** *towards the house. He can't help but look at his daughter. He stands by the sandwich table and agonisingly stares, looks away, stares.*

Leo   Sandwiches.

Dorothy   Dad.

She pulls her skirt down.

Leo   They look . . . delicious.

Dorothy   Have one. They're for you.

Leo   I'll just . . .

Leo *takes a sandwich. He leaves.* **Martin** *has been watching. He waits till* **Leo** *is indoors. He goes over to the table and picks up a sandwich. He stares at* **Dorothy**. *He goes over to her and lifts her skirt.*

Martin   Nice cunt.

Dorothy *stops him.*

Dorothy   Don't.

Martin   Shame you're wearing pants.

Dorothy   Martin.

Martin   You don't think of your sister having a cunt, do you? Barbie-smooth, you imagine. Surprising.

Dorothy   Stop it.

Martin   Nice though. If that's what you like. Let him have a good look, did you?

Dorothy   He wasn't looking.

Martin   I just saw him.

Dorothy   Leave it, Martin.

Martin   It's understandable I suppose, at his age, no harm in a look.

Dorothy   Don't say that.

Martin   I can see the attraction. You sat there. So secretarial. So available.

Dorothy   What does that mean?

Martin   Does he do it at work? When you take dictation?

Dorothy   You've got a warped mind.

Martin   To think I sprang from his loins. Made of the same stuff. The scientists are baffled.

Dorothy   Please.

Martin (*taking another sandwich*)   Did you make these?

Dorothy   Yes.

Martin   I'm going to be a chef. I've been thinking about it. In France. I'll get taught. It's an admired art in France you know. Cuisine. Means kitchen and cooking. Same word. I think I might be a bastard.

Dorothy   You are.

Martin   No, really. An actual bastard. I think mum fucked someone else. I'm not like him, am I? Do you think I'm like him?

Dorothy   Yes.

Martin   No, I'm not. I'm like mum.

Dorothy   Why do you have to say such horrible things about him?
Why do you have to attack him?

Martin   I'm not attacking him.

Dorothy   You are. He thinks you avoid him.

Martin   I do.

Dorothy   He notices. He gets hurt. He wants this to work.

Martin   Dorothy, I came home because I ran out of money.
No other reason.
A business arrangement.
. . .
Does that shock you?

Dorothy   If you just try, Martin.

Martin   It shocks me.

Leo enters. *He is carrying a deckchair and a whisky.*

Leo   Thought I'd take the sun.
Catch the last of it.
Lovely sandwiches.

Martin   I made them.

Leo   Did you?

Dorothy   I made them.

Leo   Still . . .

Martin   Have one.

Leo   No. I'm . . . not for me.

Martin   You said they were lovely.

Leo   Yes, they are. I mean. I meant they look lovely. Well done.

Martin   I'm thinking of setting up a sandwich bar.

Dorothy   Martin.

Martin   These are a sort of trial run. A place in the West End. Don't you think?

Dorothy   He's joking.

Martin   Sandwiches for offices, for people just passing by, someone's shopping, they're a bit peckish, they might fancy a sandwich. A BLT . . .

Dorothy   I made them.

Martin   B for bacon, L for lettuce and T for tomato. It's American.

Dorothy   He knows that.

Martin   The classic sandwich. Go on. Try one.

Leo   No. Thank you.

Martin   It's a good idea though, isn't it? Gap in the market.

Leo   It's not a good idea, Martin, it's rubbish.
Can we please stop talking about this? It's a perfect afternoon. I don't want to argue on a perfect afternoon.

Martin   Who's arguing? What's the argument?

Dorothy   Stop it.

Leo   Why don't we just . . . enjoy the sun together? Martin, get yourself a chair, why don't you have a drink?

Leo *strips to the waist and settles into the deckchair. He closes his eyes.*
Dorothy *clutches herself suddenly, as though a wave of nausea has passed over her.*

Martin   Don't.
Don't do that.
It doesn't make any difference when you do that.
You always do that.
It's your oldest trick.

Leo's *eyes are open although neither* **Dorothy** *nor* **Martin** *notice.*

Dorothy   I'm not . . . doing. I just . . .

Martin   I said it didn't make any difference.

Dorothy   Martin.

She reaches for him as she recovers. She tries to steady herself.

Martin   Look at you.

Martin *leaves.*

Leo   Are you all right?

Dorothy   What?
. . .
Oh. Me? Fine. Yes. Just a bit . . . You know. Indigestion.
That's all.

Leo   I shouldn't have shouted at him, I just get, when he babbles like that I get . . .
. . .
I offered him the job, you know.

Dorothy   He told me.

Leo   I think he's interested.

Dorothy   We were talking about it just now.

Leo   What did he say?

Dorothy   He said he thought it was good . . . a good idea.

Leo   He likes the idea?

Dorothy He said he thought it was, an interesting business arrangement.

Leo He would be good at it, you know, he doesn't think so but he could do it . . . He only needs to . . . get to grips with himself. He's still drifting but if I can . . . now that he's come home if we can bring him in . . . give him some . . . solidity. He said he used to play with the models. When he was little. I'd forgotten that . . .

Dorothy We could all work together.

Leo No more big projects. That's what I said to him. I'm tired of big projects . . . they run away from you. We'll stay small . . . keep everything under control.
Do you enjoy working for me, Dorothy?

Dorothy What do you mean?

Leo Do you like it?

Dorothy I love it. I mean. It's fine. It's good.

Leo You do the mail, don't you?

Dorothy Mostly. Why?

Leo And my calls. Do you answer the phone usually or does Sylvia?

Dorothy Have I done something wrong?

Leo I'm just asking.

Dorothy If there's a mistake I'll . . .

Leo There's no mistake.
I was just asking . . . just thinking.

Dorothy Tell me.

Leo I don't know what I'd do without you. That's all.
I was just thinking.
I don't know what I'd do without you.

Lights down.

4

Darkness. The quiet dripping sound of a gents public toilet. **Martin** *stands at a urinal with an empty Jenners' bag next to him* . . .

5

The roar of motorway traffic. **Dorothy** *standing beside a motorway at night. Her thumb out for a lift. Cars and lorries thunder past.*

6

Leo *and* **Paulina** *in their bedroom.* **Paulina** *looking in the mirror.*

Leo   He said he was interested . . . He seems . . . when he talks sense . . . I think we're making progress . . . Paulina?

Paulina   Hmm?

Leo   You've been sitting there for half an hour.

Paulina   I'm looking at my face.
It's changed.

Leo   It doesn't change when you look at it. It changes when you look away. Get dressed. We need to go . . .

Paulina   Leo. I don't want to go.

Leo   What?

Paulina   I never said I wanted to go.

Leo   I've bought tickets . . . There's people expecting us.

Paulina   I've heard it's terrible.
Makes no sense apparently.
Apparently it's the product of a diseased imagination.
I don't want to wallow in it.

Leo   We sponsored it.
It's supposed to be important.
It's a state of the nation play.

Paulina   I don't like tragedy.

Leo   It's farce.

Paulina   You go. If you want to go.

Leo   It's colleagues and wives. It's a colleagues and wives thing. I can't go alone.

Paulina   Stay then.

Leo   What do you want me to do? Do you want me to stay?

Paulina   Do you notice anything about the bedroom, Leo?

Leo   I'll stay if you want me to stay.

Paulina   A bed. Walls. Bedside table. Perfume. Face cream. Can you smell anything?

Leo   I can't say I noticed.

Paulina   No. You don't notice it until you notice it. Then you can't get rid of it.

Leo   I'll stay. I'll ring them and say you're ill.

7

The side of a motorway. The noise of traffic. **Dorothy** *hitching. A lorry pulls up. Its headlights flood the stage. Blinding.* **Dorothy** *gets into the lorry.*

8

The sound of dripping water. The inside of a public toilet. **Martin** *is still standing at the urinal.* **Billy** *enters. He stands near* **Martin** *at the urinal. They move together. Suddenly* **Billy** *kneels.* **Martin** *holds his head.*

9

Dorothy *and* **Joe** *in the cab of* **Joe**'s *lorry.*

Dorothy   Sometimes I want to run at the side of a house.
I get the feeling.
A red-bricked gable end.
Just turn and run at it straight. Full speed, as though it
wasn't there. Smack it and feel the bricks cut me.
Feel my skull smack.
Slide down half conscious.
Pick myself up and do it again.

Joe   Any particular house?

Dorothy   Mine. Anyone's. It doesn't matter so long as it's
made of bricks. I don't even need to be near a house to get the
feeling. I could be anywhere. At a party, in the office, in a
field and suddenly I want to smash myself against an outside
wall.

Joe   I get feelings like that sometimes.

Dorothy   Really?

Joe   All the time. In the lorry, on the motorway, now even.
I could just yank the steering wheel and twist off the road.
Plough into a bus full of schoolchildren and not stop.

He turns his hand on the steering wheel.

Just that.

He repeats the movement.

That's all it would take.
It's quite common to feel that, among lorry drivers.

Dorothy   Something stops you though?

Joe   Not much. The skin of the milk. Not much more than
that. There was a lorry driver once. It was famous. He was
driving his lorry across the Sahara Desert and he crashed . . .
right into a tree.

Dorothy   I thought there weren't any trees in the Sahara
Desert.

Joe   Only one. That's the point of the story. He crashes into
the most isolated tree in the world. Nothing but emptiness

and sand for thousands of miles in any direction and there's
this tree and he hits it. Killed himself. Killed the tree. People
said it was insanity or coincidence or fate but I can
understand it. In the middle of the desert you see a tree, one
tree and . . .

He repeats the movement.

. . . you drive at it.
Of course you do.

Dorothy   You shouldn't be allowed on the road.

Joe   All drivers get it. Coach drivers particularly. You
wouldn't become a coach driver unless you were fascinated
by death. It's all they talk about. Still. I don't want to worry
you. Touch wood.

*He touches **Dorothy**'s leg, momentarily.*

How far are you going?

Dorothy   As far as you're going. Somewhere far away. As
far away as possible.

Joe   Hull. And back.

Dorothy   Hull then.

10

*The gents toilet. In a cubicle. **Billy** is standing inside the Jenners'
bag, his face turned against the wall. **Martin** is behind him with his
hands between his legs. **Billy** turns round to kiss **Martin**.*

Martin   No.

Billy   Go on.

Martin   No.

Martin *almost pushes **Billy** away.*

11

Leo *eating*. **Paulina** *watching. Silence.*

Leo   This is nice.

Paulina   Do you think so?

Leo   Really.
Good.
Home cooking.

Paulina   I bought it.

Leo   Shame the kids . . .
Seems silly to call them kids . . .
Doesn't seem the right word, does it?
Shame they couldn't eat with us.
We should eat together more. As a family.
If I'd known we . . . I'd have asked . . .

Paulina   They're out. Didn't say where.

Leo   A family dinner. Now Martin's home. Everyone
round the table. Do the washing up together . . . like we used
to.

Paulina   Shut your mouth, Leo.

Leo   What?

Paulina   When you're eating. Shut your mouth.

Leo   Sorry.

Paulina   You always do it.
Have you noticed that?
You don't think I need to see what's in your mouth. I cooked
it. I don't need a display.

Leo   It's delicious. Very well made. It should be on display.
Why don't you have some wine?

Paulina   No.

Leo *pours himself a glass.*

Leo   You remember Eden Court? Paulina?
The housing estate I did . . . for the council . . .
'71 I think, feels like yesterday of course,
Martin was just born.

A woman came to me today.
She wants it blown up.

Paulina   Are you having an affair?

Leo   ...
I'm sorry?

Paulina   Have you had one? Recently?

Leo   What makes you think ...

Paulina   I'm asking.

Leo   No. No. I haven't, Paulina. No.
...
I'm not having an affair.

Paulina   You wouldn't tell me if you were.

Leo   Is there some kind of problem here, you don't believe
me?

Paulina   You were chatting. You usually chat to me when
you feel guilty about something.

Leo   For God's sake. I was talking about work.

Paulina   I don't know how you can drink that.

Leo   I said they want to demolish Eden Court.

Paulina   They tread on them. The grapes.

Leo   A thing I built. They want to destroy it.

Paulina   There's probably sweat in it.

Leo   I thought you'd want to know. That's all.

Paulina   Foot diseases and whatever else.

Leo   It's traditional. Traditionally that's how they make
wine.

Paulina   It turns my stomach.

Leo   It's a typical attitude, of course. Blame the architect.
People are poor. Blame the architect. Place is a slum, blame
the architect. They fill a place with pigs and then complain
it's turned into a pigsty.

Paulina   They probably urinate, the treaders, for revenge.

Leo   What?

Paulina   Revenge. They probably laugh as it runs down their legs.

Leo   I don't think so.

Paulina   You don't know what goes on in a person's mind.

Leo   It's good wine.

Paulina   All sorts of thoughts.

Leo   I thought you liked claret.

Paulina   Shut your mouth, Leo, you're doing it again . . .

Leo   I never understand the point of table manners you know. Fork this side, fork that side. It's all class. There's no beauty in it. No truth. Do you know, in some countries, if you're enjoying a meal, it's considered polite to belch. When I was in Saudi . . .

Paulina   If you want to belch go into the garden.

Leo   I don't want to belch, I'm just saying . . .

Paulina   Make your noises there.

Leo   I'm making a point. Table manners aren't . . .

Paulina   Excuse me.

Paulina *gets up and leaves.*

Leo   Paulina!
Paulina.
. . .

He pours another glass. Lights a cigarette.

12

Billy *and* **Martin** *in the streets.* **Billy** *walks behind* **Martin**. **Martin** *is trying to shake him off.*

Billy   Mister. Oi. Mister. Wait.

Martin ...

Billy *catches up with him.*

Billy Billy.

Martin What d'you want?

Billy What's your name.

Martin None of your fucking business.

Billy Just asking.

Martin If I'd wanted you to know my name I'd tell you it.
Wouldn't I?

Billy I know but ...

Martin So stop following me.

Billy I've never seen you there before.
You're new.
Usually old blokes ...

Martin *begins to move off.* **Billy** *follows him.*

Billy Married ... pot bellies and smelly dicks.
You're not married, are you ...

Martin I told you to fucking stop.

Billy *points to a shop window. In the shop window is a green jacket on
a stand.*

Billy Have you seen this jacket.

Martin You keep talking to me.

Billy It's like that jacket. You know, the one John Wayne
wore in *The Quiet Man*.

Martin Stop it.

Billy You'd suit green, you'd look good in it.

Martin I'm going to walk away. If you follow me I'm
going to run. If you keep following me I'm going to punch
you.

Billy D'you promise?

Martin   I'll hit your face and I'll keep hitting it until you
leave me alone. You don't want that, do you?

Billy   Are you rich? You look quite rich. Are you?

Martin   ...

Billy   Your accent. You could probably buy that jacket. As
a present to yourself.

Martin   I warned you ...

Martin *approaches* **Billy** *as if about to hit him.* **Billy** *suddenly
turns and punches through the glass of the shop window.*

13

Paulina *and* **Leo**. *The phone rings.* **Paulina** *has returned.*

Leo   No comment.
No comment.
I'm sorry.
I've told you no comment.
The buildings are structurally sound.
That's all I'm prepared to say at the moment.
No comment.
Thank you.
Goodbye.
Fucking idiot.
...
Newspaper.
You should eat something.

Paulina   No.

Leo   You're making yourself ill.

Paulina   Just the thought of it. I can't.

Leo   It's a chicken, Paulina, just chicken.

Paulina   I saw a programme about it.

Leo   Perfectly good food.

Paulina   Probably riddled with disease.

Leo It looks fine to me. You cooked it.

Paulina If you had an affair you wouldn't tell me, would you?

Leo *puts some food on a plate and pushes it towards her.*

Paulina No.

Leo You're not turning vegetarian on me, are you?

Paulina Maybe. Maybe I'll stop eating altogether.

Leo I'm not having an affair, Paulina. Now eat something.

Paulina Fruit. I'll be fruitarian.

Leo Jesus.

Paulina I couldn't plan for it. If you had an affair. I wouldn't know until it had happened.

Leo It won't happen.

Paulina You'd disguise your guilt by paying me more attention.

Leo Don't be stupid.

Paulina You could infect me. I wouldn't know. I couldn't plan for it.

Leo Christ, Paulina, you're like a needle picking at a splinter. Jab jab jab. We're having dinner. I don't need this kind of . . . this . . . whatever it is you're trying to prove . . . Can't you just . . . Make small talk, be normal, eat the chicken, for God's sake . . .

Paulina The thought of bird flesh. Rotting inside me.

Leo Why did you cook it then?
Why did you cook the fucking thing if you didn't want to eat it?

Paulina Habit, probably.
. . .
I'm sorry.

Pause. **Paulina**, *still, quietly, begins to weep.* **Leo** *goes to her, stands behind her and holds her.*

Leo   Is something wrong? Did I say something? Paulina, what's the matter?

Paulina   Pesticides on fruit.

Leo   Paulina.

Paulina   The rain rains on it. Washes the chemicals off.

Leo   Love.

Paulina   And then the rain's dirty. Full of poison.

Leo *tries to kiss her neck.*

Leo   Please don't cry.

Paulina   Don't leave me, Leo.
Don't go away.

Leo   I'm not going anywhere.

Paulina   They've gone. Don't you go too.

14

A Country Kitchen motorway service station. **Dorothy** *and* **Joe** *are sitting at a table. Their chairs are fixed to the floor. The light is sterile. It is dark outside.* **Joe** *is drinking tea from a jumbo-sized paper cup.* **Dorothy** *has been sleeping.*

Dorothy   What time is it?

Joe   Late. Nearly home. I bought you a tea.

Dorothy   Thank you.

Joe (*sings*)   It's four in the morning and once more the dawning . . .
. . .
Don't you want it?

Dorothy   No. How close are we?

Joe   An hour or so.
It'll get cold. You should drink it.

A nice hot cup of tea.
Do you good. Rinse out the insides.

Dorothy   I don't like tea.

Joe   Everyone likes tea. Except snobs.
You're not a coffee drinker, are you?

Dorothy   I just feel a bit . . .
You know . . . a bit.

Joe   I thought you might be thirsty, that's all.

Dorothy *clutches herself. A wave of nausea passes over her.*

Joe   Are you all right?

Dorothy   Yes.

Joe   You don't seem it.

Dorothy   I'm fine. It's finished now.

Joe   Moaning and groaning.

Dorothy   Honestly. I know what it is. It's gone now.
Honestly.

Joe   Are you sure you don't want some tea?

Dorothy   No.

Joe   It's still warm. They gave me a jumbo cup.
They know me here. I'm a regular.
I always stop and I always have a jumbo.
I don't even have to ask.
The girls just know.
Do your parents know where you are?

Dorothy   No.

Joe   They must be worried.

Dorothy   No.

Joe   I'm sorry. I don't mean to pry. Only I get runaways.
Hitching. You feel responsible.

Dorothy   I just needed to get away. I'm not . . . it's just
something I do from time to time. No one worries.

Joe   If your father got hold of me he'd go mad. Wouldn't he? If he could see us now?

Dorothy   He won't notice.

Joe   You've been away all night.

Dorothy   I'll be back in the morning.
Where are we now?

Joe   Junction 17.

Dorothy   What are we carrying?

Joe   Barbed wire. Sheet metal. Fences. Security gear.

Dorothy   Are we nearly there?

Joe   If you look out that window you can see the lights of the skyscrapers, the tallest ones. See . . . that's forty miles away. Forty miles. Amazing. Would he go mad? Your father?

Dorothy   What's in between?

Joe   What?

Dorothy   Here and there.

Joe   Road.

Dorothy   There must be more than just road.

Joe   Well. Road and . . .
Obviously there's towns.

Dorothy   Which ones?

Joe   Small ones. You know. More suburbs in fact. Suburbs you'd call them.
. . .
And fields I suppose.

Dorothy   What do they grow?

Joe   Cows I think. Mainly. It's cows you see anyway.

Dorothy *wipes her face with a napkin. She examines the napkin.*

Dorothy   How long was I asleep?

Joe Most of the way. You just curled up on the seat.

Dorothy I'm sorry.

Joe Why?

Dorothy I didn't chat. I slept.

Joe I drive a truck. I'm used to my own company.
I wouldn't say I enjoy it but I tolerate it.
I'm like an old married couple. I tolerate myself.

Dorothy It was warm. You had the heater on. I couldn't keep my eyes open. I always sleep best in trucks.

Joe Did you dream?

Dorothy No dreams.

Joe You looked peaceful. Nice.

Dorothy I'm sorry I slept. It wasn't what you wanted.

Joe I enjoyed your presence. That was company enough. As a matter of fact it's nice to have a girl beside you as you drive. Do your parents know where you go? When you're on these trips?

Dorothy They never ask.

Joe With a boyfriend?

Dorothy Probably.

Joe Don't they want to meet him? Talk to him?

Dorothy We don't have that in our family.

Joe What?

Dorothy Asking. Telling.

Joe Still.

Dorothy What do you mean nice?

Joe . . .

Dorothy Nice to have a girl.

Joe I didn't mean to offend you. Any man would . . . would feel . . .

Dorothy   What?

Joe   It doesn't matter. I shouldn't have said.

Dorothy   Go on.

Joe   Just having a girl near you. Your skin on the seat. Your breathing. That's all.

Dorothy   Tell me.

Joe   You know.

Dorothy   Say.

Joe   Any man would. A girl.

Dorothy   I turned you on?

Joe   No.
Yes.
No. Not 'turned on'. That's not the right words.

Dorothy   What then.

Joe   Moved. I was moved.

Dorothy   In what way?

Joe   Powerfully.

Dorothy   Powerfully in what way?

Joe   This is stupid. Just forget I said anything.

Dorothy   I want to know.

Joe   It's a mixture of things . . . a man's feelings . . . they . . . you become sort of . . . full of . . . wanting.

Dorothy   Wanting.

Joe   Please don't take offence.

Dorothy   I won't.

Joe   You want to . . . you know . . . touch her. Hold her breasts in your . . . see her . . . you know.

Dorothy   Oh.

Joe   But then I felt something different.

Dorothy   What?

Joe   Sadness. I felt sad for you.

Dorothy   And . . .

Joe   Then I felt sad for me.

Dorothy   And.

Joe   Then I felt sad for us. For everybody.
Funny, isn't it?
. . .
I wanted to hold you.

Dorothy   Why?

Joe   I wanted to protect you. From men like me.

Dorothy   Is that all?

Joe   You're not revolted?

Dorothy   No.

Joe   You don't mind me saying things like this?

Dorothy   It's what I want.

Joe   My wife would never let me say things like this to her.

Dorothy   You could tell her.

Joe   You don't want your wife to know you have these
thoughts. This. Me. Here. You. My heart thumping like this.
A young woman. I couldn't stand it if she knew these things
about me. Looking at girls. Looking at you. I mean. I love
my wife.

Dorothy   Do you?

Joe   Not love exactly. Care. No. It's hard to know the
word. There's a connection between a man and his wife. You
can't break it. Sometimes I think she knows what's
disgusting about me. You think she can read your mind.
Horrible. But you never say anything. You just couldn't.
. . .
We should stop. Talking about this stuff.

Dorothy   We can stop if you want to.
Do you want to?

Joe   No. It's all right.
. . .
Ask more.

Dorothy   Do you look at your wife? When she's asleep?

Joe   I used to but . . . your wife . . . it would be like looking at your mother.

Dorothy   Did you do anything else? Apart from look at me?

Joe   No.
Not really.

Dorothy   Say.

Joe   I didn't do anything.

Dorothy   You said . . .

Joe   I tried to touch you. I reached out my hand to . . .
Lift your . . .
But I didn't. I could feel you breathing on my fingertips.
Common decency to stop. Or fear. Skin of the milk. I wanted to. Nearly fainted from it.
Why do you want to know all this?

Dorothy   Why do you want to tell me?

15

The urgent sound of an alarm. **Billy** *and* **Martin** *on the street by the smashed shop window.* **Billy** *is holding the green jacket. His hand is bleeding.*

Billy   For you.

Martin   You smashed it.

Billy   Put it on.

Martin   Put your fist through a fucking window. Jesus.

Billy   Put it on. Go on. It's a present.

Martin   Wait. Billy . . .

Billy   You said Billy.

Martin   I don't want presents. I don't want to know who you are. All I want is for you to go away. You go that way and I'll go this way. Please.

Billy   Made a brilliant noise. Didn't it? Crash.

Martin   You shouldn't have done it.

Billy   Take it. Take the jacket. It's yours.

Martin   I don't want it. You have it.

Billy   I chose it for you.

Martin *takes the jacket.* **Billy** *sits down on the pavement.*

Martin   Thank you.

Billy   Wear it.

Martin   Your hand.

Billy   Wear it.

Martin   You're cut.

Billy   It's a beautiful jacket. Wear it.

Martin *puts the jacket on.*

Billy   Give us a twirl.

Martin   Can you run? You run that way. Let's just run. We'll leave the jacket and run.

Billy *is sitting by the smashed window. His hand is bleeding.*
Martin *tears a strip off the bottom of his shirt and gives it to* **Billy**.

Martin   Wrap that round your hand.

Billy   What's this? Guess this? (*American accent.*) For a minute there I thought we were in trouble.

Martin   I don't want to know.

Billy (*American accent*)   For a minute there I thought we . . .

Martin   Please. I'm asking. Run.

Billy   Can you guess it?

Martin   Will you run, you mad cunt?

Billy   Right. We're surrounded, by hundreds and
hundreds of Mexican police, you're bandaging my hand . . .
Can you guess it . . . ?

Martin   Why are you doing this?

Billy (*American*)   Wait a minute. Did you hear something?

Martin   Where?

Billy   No. It's part of the film. You have to guess.

Martin   Billy.

Billy (*American*)   For a minute there I thought we were in
trouble.

Billy *enacts the final moment from* Butch Cassidy and the
Sundance Kid. *He stands up, ready to spring into action, guns
blazing and just as he comes out of the imaginary building he freezes
and makes the sound of thousands of guns going off.*

Martin *puts his hand over* **Billy**'s *mouth. Eventually lets go of him.*

Billy   *Butch Cassidy and the Sundance Kid.*
Final scene. I videoed it off the telly.
That looks a bit tight around the arms, you know.
Do you want a size larger?

Martin   All right. You win. I know a place. We'll go there.
Let's just get out of here before the police come.

Billy   Where? Your place?

Martin   Just a place I know. Near here. I go sometimes.
Come on.

Billy *is looking at his reflection in what remains of the shop window.*

Billy   Look at us. You be Sundance. I'll be Butch.

Martin   Let's just go.

Billy (*American*) Whaddaya mean you can't swim? The fall'll probably kill ya.

Martin Hurry up.

Billy *takes* **Martin**'s *hand. Pretends to jump off a cliff.*

Billy Whooooooaaaaaaah.

Looking at their reflection **Billy** *kisses* **Martin** *sexually.*

Martin Billy.
Billy.
What are you doing?
Don't.

He pushes **Billy** *off him.*

What the fuck do you think I am?
Christ.

16

Leo *and* **Paulina**. *A dim light.* **Paulina** *is clearing up dinner plates and wiping.*

Leo When we were first together.

She wipes around him.

I thought you were the most beautiful thing I'd ever seen.

Paulina Are you finished?

Leo Oh. Yes. Thank you.
Everything about you was perfect and I made sure to keep you. I thought about you all the time. About how things would be? About what I'd do . . .

She goes into the kitchen. **Leo** *lights a cigarette.*

But you start with things, you draw up plans and then they get confused. People spoil things and . . . time and you lose the clarity. So you have to get back to the original . . . go back to the drawing board . . .

. . .

We'll get out of the city. Paulina. A village somewhere. We'll do up a house or something. I'll work from the attic. Get back to the original us . . . all of us . . . You, me, Dorothy, Martin . . .

Paulina   You're smoking.

Leo   You know, Paulina, you're still a lovely looking woman.

Paulina   Put it out.

Leo   For your age. Considering. You are.

Paulina   I said you weren't to smoke here.

Leo   I want to smoke. It's a lovely night. I've had a lovely meal. Stars in a black sky and this is my lovely wife.

Paulina *takes the cigarette from his hand and stubs it out.*

Leo   I look at you sometimes and I think, I can see you when you were twenty-two . . . when I first . . .

Paulina   You said you wouldn't do that.

Leo   I can see the original, and I think . . . I want to say . . .

Paulina   Not in the house. I asked you.

Leo   I know you don't like me saying it but . . .

Paulina   Fumes and . . .

Leo   It doesn't stop me from wanting to say it.

Paulina   Dirt and . . .

Leo   I look at you and I want to say . . .
You're a beautiful woman.

Paulina   Ashes and . . .

Leo   It's pleasant just to sit here and look at you.

Paulina   Stop it, Leo.

Leo   I mean it.

Paulina   Stop.

Leo I want to say it. I feel it.
It's objectively true.
You're beautiful.

Paulina Leo.

Leo My beautiful wife.

Paulina *throws a plate down onto the floor, it breaks.*

Leo Paulina!

Paulina Don't call me that.

Leo Well, what do you want me to call you then?

Paulina At the moment, nothing.

Leo I have to call you something. I can't just point at you.

Paulina I don't want you to refer to me.
. . .

Leo I'm sorry. I should have offered to help with the clearing up.
. . .
Paulina, what's wrong?

Paulina I said not to smoke.

Leo I know, love, but after a meal, I like to . . .

Paulina Why did I do that?

Leo You were upset. It's understandable. I'm sorry.

Paulina Plate throwing. It's so . . . domestic.

Leo I'll clear it up. You sit down.

Paulina So banal.

Leo, *on his hands and knees starts to pick up pieces of plate.* **Paulina** *sits.*

Leo You snapped. That's all. What with Martin coming home and . . . I've not been in the best of moods. I've not helped. You snapped. It's probably a good thing.

Paulina Such a poor gesture.

Leo   The thing is . . . we need to get things clear between us.
I've let you drift away from me. We don't communicate. The
two of us. In our own worlds. But we're lucky. That's what
we have to remember. We're the lucky ones. We have
everything . . . that's what's important to remember.

*He is now standing behind her. He tries to kiss her. Her resistance is
tired.*

You feel so good.

Paulina   Leo.

Leo   So soft.

Paulina   Go to bed.

Leo   So lovely.

*He starts trying to undress her. She is stiff. Corpse-like, she gives
nothing. He continues. He kisses her breasts. She holds his head. She
tolerates him.*

So lovely. Such a beautiful woman. So beautiful.

17

Joe *and* **Dorothy** *in the motorway service station.*

Joe   I've got a confession to make.

Dorothy   Go on.

Joe   In the cab. I was listening to country music. Do you
like country music?

Dorothy   I don't know.

Joe   Marty Robbins? Do you know Marty Robbins? El
Paso? Devil Woman? White Sport Coat?
(*Sings.*) 'A white sport coat, and a pink carnation . . . I'm all
dressed up, for the dance.'

Dorothy   Is that your confession?

Joe   I was listening to the song and . . .
. . .

I touched myself.
I didn't touch you.
One hand was reaching over to touch you but with the other
I unzipped and . . .

Dorothy Who was driving the lorry for God's sake?

Joe We were stopped. Out there, in the lorry park. I
couldn't bear to wake you up.

. . .
Are you sure you don't want some tea?

Dorothy Sure.

Joe You could have me arrested.

Dorothy Could I?

Joe Sent to prison.

Dorothy I've only got your word for it. I didn't see
anything.

Joe But I confessed.

Dorothy People confess all the time. It means nothing.
Hardened criminals confess to cover their tracks.

Joe Do you feel violated?

Dorothy Do you want me to?

Joe . . .
Yes.

Dorothy *doubles up again, holding herself as before.*

Joe What's wrong?

Dorothy I get attacks. It's nothing.

Joe Attacks? Attacks of what?

Dorothy Dread. Don't laugh at me.

Joe I'd never.

Dorothy I get signals. Messages. Warnings. I'm not
mental.

Joe Of course you're not.

Dorothy   Can we leave?

Joe   It could be . . . you know . . . woman-related. You've all sorts of organs down there. It could be any one of them.

Dorothy   Let's go to the lorry. Please.

Joe   These signals. Do you know where they come from?

Dorothy   No.

Joe   Maybe it's my fault.

Dorothy   No.

Joe   Maybe I'm signalling you. Maybe that's what you've been receiving. I felt something. All night maybe I've been sending out signals. Like dolphin calls across the ocean floor. Perhaps it's something like that . . .

He demonstrates.

Poooooooooooow . . . Poooooooooooooow . . . Poooooooooooow

Dorothy *laughs.*

Dorothy   Must be different frequencies, Joe. It's not your signals I'm getting. Your signals must be being picked up somewhere else.

18

Billy *and* **Martin** *on the roof of a tall building. Night.* **Billy** *is tuning a small radio. He moves around the roof searching for a signal.* **Martin** *is sitting on the edge of the roof, his legs dangling into space. Below, there is a carpet of lights stretching into the far distance. The sounds of the city float up from below, less like real noises than like memories of noises.*

The radio picks up crackles and whines, snatches of music. Eventually **Billy** *settles on a signal. A pop song. He loses it and changes position. He gains the signal again by balancing on the edge of the roof. Precariously. We hear the first bars of 'Take Me Home Country Roads' by John Denver.* **Billy** *is absolutely still . . .*

Billy Listen.

Martin Shhh.

Billy Listen.

Martin Shhh.

Billy Martin . . .

Martin Billy.

19

A garden in the suburbs. The wind blowing gently. Suddenly
Paulina *enters in some distress. She gags, holding her hand over her*
mouth. She goes further into the garden. She vomits.

20

The roof with **Billy** *and* **Martin***, as before.*

Billy Almost heaven . . .

Martin *tries to keep his composure.*

Billy West Virginia.

Martin Billy.

Billy Blue Ridge Mountains.

Martin Don't sing.

Billy Shenandoah River.

Martin I said, don't sing.

Billy Life is old there.

Martin Please.

Billy Older than the trees.

Martin Switch it off.

Billy Younger than the mountains.

Martin   I come here for quiet.

Billy   Growing in the breeze.

Martin *tries to snatch the radio,* **Billy** *holds it out over the edge.*

Billy   Take me home.

Martin   It's supposed to be quiet.

Billy   Country roads.

Martin   You're spoiling it.

Billy   To the place.

Martin   Billy!

Billy   That I belong.

Martin   You're spoiling everything.

Billy   West Virginia.

Martin   Give me that fucking thing.

Billy   Mountain momma.

Martin   I'm warning you.

Billy   Take me home.

Martin *punches* **Billy** *hard.*

Billy   Fuck.

Billy *totters on the edge.* **Martin** *catches him. The radio falls.*

21

The garden. **Paulina** *stands in darkness, recovering.* **Leo** *enters.*

Leo   Paulina.
Where are you?
Are you there?
Paulina.
Paulina.

22

The back of a container lorry. **Dorothy** *and* **Joe** *in a half light, surrounded by barbed wire and security equipment.*

Dorothy   It's cold.

Joe   I'm sorry.

Dorothy   Isn't there any heating?

Joe   In the cab. This is just the container.

Dorothy   What's all this stuff?

Joe   Deliveries.

Dorothy   Barbed wire?

Joe   For building sites. Stops vandals. Kids'll nick anything these days. If it's not nailed down.

Dorothy   Joe . . .

Joe   If you don't want to . . .

Dorothy   I don't know.

Joe   We don't have to. We can go.

Dorothy   Kiss me.

Joe   Are you sure?

Dorothy   No.

Joe *approaches her. Cautiously he touches her face.*

Dorothy   Do you want me? Really?

Joe   Yes.

Dorothy   Say it.

Joe   I want you.

Dorothy   Don't touch me.

Joe   But . . . you said to . . .

Dorothy   Stand back. Stand there.

Joe   I'm sorry . . . I didn't mean to upset you . . .

Dorothy   Look at me.

A pause.

Dorothy   Do you think I'm available?

Joe   I shouldn't have asked you to do this.

Dorothy   It's an important question, Joe. Do you think I'm available?

Joe   No. Of course not.

Dorothy   It's important. Available, Joe.

Joe   ... Yes. I don't know.

Dorothy   Look at me. What is it about me? What gives you feelings? Tell me.

Joe   This is wrong, Dorothy. This isn't working. You said you wanted ... My wife ...

Dorothy   Is it the clothes?

She starts to take off her dress.

Joe   Please don't.

It's cold. She holds herself awkwardly.

Dorothy   Say you want me.

Joe   I want you.

Dorothy   Say I'm yours.

Joe   You're mine.

Dorothy   What does it feel like?

Joe   Dorothy.

Dorothy   Important, Joe. What does it feel like?

Joe   I ... you're ... this is embarrassing, Dorothy.

Dorothy   You. Now. Tell me the feeling.

Joe   I feel ashamed. I feel disgusted.

Dorothy   By me?

Joe   This isn't what I imagined. You asked me to come with you. You seemed sure. I didn't mean . . . now you turn round and start this. I thought you . . .

You talked to me, didn't you?

Listened.

You wanted me.

Everything was like a dream come true and now this.

Now you're all . . .

All . . .

Dorothy   What? All what?

Joe   Just get dressed.

Dorothy   Is it my body?

Joe   Please.

Dorothy   Is my body wrong?

Joe   No.

Dorothy   Don't you want to look at it?

Joe   Not like this.

Dorothy   How then? Like this?

She takes up a page-three pose. No smile.

Joe   No!

Dorothy   You have to say. You have to tell me. How do you want me to be? How Joe?

She doubles up again. He approaches her. Holds her. Covers her up. She remains still.

23

Leo and **Paulina** *in the garden. Dark.* **Leo** *smoking.* **Paulina** *standing apart.*

Leo   This isn't going to happen, Paulina.

Paulina   I want you to put concrete over the grass.

Leo   I won't lose you.
You have to . . .
We both . . .

Paulina   I don't want grass.

Leo   All of us have to stop this . . . falling apart that's
happening here.

Paulina   I want a patio.

Leo   This is my family.
Families have problems. It's natural. You expect it.

Paulina   Leave a space for the roses.

Leo   But you can't just . . .
You have to pull things back together.

Paulina   All the rest concrete.

24

The roof. **Billy** *and* **Martin**.

Martin   Sorry.

Billy   Been hit worse before.

Martin   You kept going . . . you . . .

Billy   Not even a hit really. A slap it was. Not a punch. I've
had it harder than that.

Martin   I don't hit people. Not normally. Not for pleasure.

Billy   It was all right.

Martin   Don't.

Billy   Motherly, almost.

Martin   For God's sake.

Billy   Warm. Nice.

Martin   I said I was sorry.

Billy   No need.

Martin   I come up here to get away from . . . for silence.
Because it's pure. No voices. No talking.

Billy   I came up for you. I'm the one who should be sorry.

Martin   Twenty floors up you'd think there'd be nothing.
No people, no sound, no signals, no feelings.
And then you.
I had it. Just for a moment.
And then you.

Billy   I spoiled it.

Martin   Blankness. Purity. And then that trash.

Billy   Steady on. I like John Denver.

Martin   That isn't the point.

Billy   I think John Denver is pure.

Martin   Pollution.

Billy   Looks almost like the Milky Bar kid.

Martin   We could have fucked.
We could have.
Us, alone, no mess.
You spoiled it.

Billy   You're upset.

Martin   Yes.

Billy   I thought it was how we were feeling.
I thought it was romantic. Our song.
I've always wanted an 'our song' with someone.
We could have danced.
Like in a film.

Martin   I don't want something that's like in a film.
Something that's like in a film is exactly what I don't want.
I wanted to slip away.

Billy   From what?

Martin   You. Me. Everything.

Billy   If you'd told me.

Martin   It was a perfect moment.

Billy   There'll be another. They probably happen all the time up here. Regular.

Martin   What do you know about perfect moments?

Billy   I know.

Martin   How?

Billy   I just had one then.

25

The inside of the lorry. The engine is turning over. **Dorothy** *and* **Joe** *are parked outside her house.*

Dorothy   I'd better go.

Joe   ...

Dorothy   I've got work tomorrow.

Joe   ...

Dorothy   I'm sorry it didn't ...
I'm sorry I wasn't ...

Joe   ...

Dorothy   You weren't to know about me.
I don't know about me.
I'm not nice.
I led you on. Didn't I?

Joe   ...

Dorothy   Will you see me again? Send signals.
Poooooooow ...
Will you stop for me?

Joe   ...

Dorothy   Goodbye, Joe.

She kisses his cheek and gets out of the cab.

We see **Paulina** *standing in the garden.*

We see **Leo**.

We see **Billy** *and* **Martin** *standing on the roof.* **Martin** *is standing behind* **Billy** *holding his head.*

Leo I won't let you drift away, Paulina.

Billy You can see my house from here.

Leo We're a good family.

Billy Martin.
I said you can see . . .

Martin *lets go of* **Billy**'*s head.*

Martin What makes you think I care where you live?

Leo I won't let you put up walls between us.

Paulina You're the architect, Leo.

Billy *suddenly turns and runs full tilt at the edge of the roof.*

Martin Billy!

Martin *tries to catch him, he has to run full speed after him. They both run towards the edge.*

Blackout.

Act Two

1

Darkness.

Lights suddenly up on **Billy** *being caught by* **Martin** *just as he is about to go over the edge.*

Martin   You cunt.

Martin *holds* **Billy**, *limply, despairing. In the background we hear a large series of explosions. The sound of applause. Lights down.*

2

Some weeks later.

The garden is in a mess. It has been dug up, ploughed and turned over. There are only scattered patches of green. A pile of concrete paving stones are stacked against the wall of the house. **Leo** *is paving over the garden.*

Paulina *enters carrying plant pots. She begins to transfer plants from the garden into pots. She watches him.*

Leo   Working.

Paulina   I can see.

Leo   It seems a shame to . . .

Paulina   It's what I want.

Leo   Yes, I know, love, but . . .

Paulina   You can sweep patios.

Leo   To cover it all though . . .

Paulina   Wash them.

Leo   It'll take value off the house.
People like a garden.

Paulina   I don't want you trailing dirt inside.

Leo   But when . . . if we move. When we go to the country . . . it seems a shame.

Paulina   Hose yourself down when you're finished.

Martin *comes out. Dressed for going out. He is wearing the green jacket.*

A pause.

Martin   You'll kill him.

Paulina   Is that what you're wearing?

Martin   I've been watching from the bedroom.

Paulina   Are you going somewhere?

Martin   All that sweating.

Paulina   Somewhere you want to attract attention?

Martin   Manual labour. He's not used to it. You'll put a strain on his heart.

Paulina   You should be careful.

Martin   I'm going out.

Paulina   Clothes send signals.

Martin   He's been at it all afternoon.

Paulina   There are people, Martin, who interpret signals. One way or another.

Martin   It's a labour of love.

Paulina   Signals attract them.

Martin   He's moving the earth for you.

Paulina   These people.

Martin   Is the earth moving for you?

Paulina   Even if you don't actually talk to them. They come into your proximity. You should be careful.

Martin   You got another spade, boss?

Leo   . . .

Martin   Give us it.

Leo   What for?

Martin   I can just see myself as a digger.

Leo *gives* **Martin** *the spade.* **Martin** *takes his jacket off. They dig together.*

Paulina   I thought you were going out.

Martin   I decided to work instead.

Leo   You could dig there if you want.

Paulina   You'll have to throw away your good clothes.

Martin   Father and son together in honest toil.

Paulina   You'll spoil them.

Martin   Good this, isn't it, boss?

Leo   What?

Martin   Digging.

Paulina   You don't both have to do it.

Martin   You and me. Digging together.

Paulina   It only means two sets of dirt.

Martin   I could dig roads in Canada or something.

Leo   You don't dig roads. You build them.

Martin   Digging's involved though. The company of digging men.

Leo   They use earth movers.

Martin   I could dig.

Leo   Nowadays road building's all about planning.

Paulina   You'll want beer.

Leo   Ask yourself what the road's for.

Paulina   When you do father and son things you always want beer.

Leo A beer would be nice.

Paulina There isn't any.

Leo You ask yourself. Who's going to use this road? Why? What do they need? How can it be more beautiful? That's what the job's about, that's what men like me, and you, are for, Martin . . . we ask questions . . . you understand?

They dig for some moments in silence.

Martin Actually, I'm bored of this.

Martin *stops.*

Leo You've only just started.

Martin Sorry.

Leo (*to* **Paulina**) I thought you were getting beers.

Martin For a minute I thought I would . . .
But then I seemed to get bored.

Leo He wants a beer.

Martin Digging wasn't that interesting after all.

Leo That's what I'm telling you. It's the planning that's interesting, the questions . . .

Martin Sorry, Boss.
Maybe I'm just not cut out for work.
I have to go.

Paulina You're not coming into the house.

Martin I'll be late.

Leo Martin.

Martin See you later.

Martin *exits through the house.*

Leo You could have given him a drink.

Paulina He didn't want a drink.

Leo Of course he did. It's a warm day. He wanted a cold beer. I want a cold beer.

Paulina   You wanted a beer. He wanted to dig.
. . .
Do you know they use fish brains in beer?

Leo   Fish heads.

Paulina   No wonder it makes people violent.
Men urinating in the street.
Women stumbling around like retarded people.
Considering what they put in it, it's no wonder.

*They hear the sound of the doorbell. Neither of them move. After a
moment* **Dorothy** *enters.*

Dorothy   There's a woman here to see you.

Leo   Who?

Paulina   A woman?

Dorothy   Mackie she said.

Leo   Christ.

Dorothy   Will I tell her you're busy?

Leo   No. No. Bring her through.

Dorothy *exits*.

Leo   Business.

Paulina   Shame.

Sheena *enters with* **Dorothy**.

Sheena   This is lovely. What a lovely house you've got, Mr
Black. Did you build it?

Leo   No.

Sheena   And this is your . . . backyard?

Dorothy   It's a patio actually.

Sheena   For sitting out?

Paulina   It's easier to clean.

Sheena   Of course it is. I'd love a patio. You don't get
much chance to sit out where I am. You must be Mrs Black.

Paulina   Paulina.

Sheena   Sheena Mackie.

Leo   You always seem to find me at weekends, Ms Mackie.

Sheena   I've got a job. I have to work in the week. And this is your daughter?

Dorothy   Dorothy.

Sheena   The girl I talked to on the phone?

Leo   Dorothy is also my secretary.

Sheena   A family business. That's nice. We hardly need introduced, do we? We've chatted so often.

Leo   Why don't you get us some tea, Dorothy? If you'll allow me to get changed, Ms Mackie, I'll be with you in a moment.

Leo *and* **Dorothy** *exit.* **Paulina** *continues potting plants.*
Sheena *stands silent.*

Paulina   I've always thought it would be nice to live in a tall building.

Sheena   Oh?

Paulina   Is it nice?

Sheena   Nice? Not really. Not nice. No.

Paulina   Are you scared of heights?

Sheena   Height's not really the problem.

Paulina   Oh no. Height's a strong point. You don't want to be in amongst it.

Sheena   Amongst it?

Paulina   Ground floors attract opportunist thieves. I don't imagine they bother with the tenth. On the tenth you can watch it all happening down below. Rise above it all. Do you watch?

Sheena   Sometimes. Sometimes I can't avoid it. Sometimes I'm in amongst it myself.

3

Billy *and* **Martin** *on top of a tall building. Daytime.* **Billy** *pointing.*

Billy   There . . . to the left.

Martin   Where?

Billy   Follow my finger.

Martin   There's only tower blocks.

Billy   That's it . . . there see.

Martin   There?

Billy   Third along.

Martin   You live there?

Billy   Yeah.

Martin   Christ.

Billy   What d'you mean, Christ?

Martin   I mean . . . Christ. Isn't it supposed to be . . . I've never been. I thought you were showing because . . .

Billy   I'm showing you because it's where I live.

Martin   I've never. I haven't seen any of those places . . . close up. I mean.

Billy   Where do you live?

Martin   You can't see it from here.

Billy   Is it a flat?

Martin   No.

Billy   A house.

Martin   Yes.

Billy   Is it detached or part of a street?

Martin   Detached. Do we have to talk about this?

Billy   Nice area?

Martin If you like nice areas.

Billy Can I visit?

Martin When I was a student I lived in a squat.

Billy Can I visit?

Martin No.

Billy *starts to walk along the edge of the roof. Calmly balancing.*

Billy Why not? You can visit me.

Martin So. Don't do that.

Billy Visit me. On my dangerous estate.

Martin You'll fall off.

Billy It's like Beirut you know. War zone.

Martin Is it?

Billy Is it fuck.

Martin I said don't do that.

Billy You're scared.

Martin Probably better than where I stay anyway.

Billy How's that?

Martin I don't know. It probably is.

Billy How's it better?

Martin The people probably. Probably the atmosphere.
Isn't it supposed to be better. Neighbours talk to each other.
I don't know. How should I know?
. . .
Will you fucking stop doing that? It makes me nervous.

Billy *stops walking along the roof edge.*

Billy Can I visit yours then?

Martin I won't be there long anyway.

Billy You moving?

Martin Leaving.

Billy   Leaving what?

Martin   Home. I can't stick it.
The city. The country. All of it.
I'm off.

Billy   Where to?

Martin   Canada. I don't know. Albania maybe. Maybe
Fife. Some wilderness. Somewhere with mountains.

Billy   A holiday?

Martin   Escape.

Billy   What have you got to escape from?

Martin   You wouldn't understand.

Billy   Maybe I would.

Martin   I need a change.

Billy   I like you as you are.

Martin   You're shit, you'll take anything.

Billy   I take what I want.

Martin   I'm fucking off. On my own. No people. No talk.
No things.

Billy   I'll come with you.

Martin   No, you won't.

Billy   Why not?

Martin   I don't want you to come.

Billy   Yes, you do.

Martin   You'd only talk. When people talk they clog your
head with shit. The shit they talk gets in your head and slops
around. More and more shit. Television schedules. Opinions
about sport. Property prices. It all slops around until
eventually it slops out your mouth and back into someone
else's head.

Billy   You're fucked up?

Martin   Course I'm fucked up.

Billy   We've got something in common then.
I'm fucked up as well.

Martin   No, you're not.

Billy   I try to run off the top of buildings.

Martin   That's natural. You're poor.
. . .
I just can't . . . I'm not . . . not any more.
. . .
I need to get pure. I got off on the wrong foot somewhere.
Somewhere around when I was born. Now I need to go back.
Go back get clean and start again.
. . .
I'm going to learn to make furniture.

Billy   I'd like to do that.

Martin   If I go to the country somewhere. I could find
some old guy in the mountains that does it.

Billy   Yeah!

Martin   An old guy with a fat old wife.

Billy   Yeah!

Martin   He might be deaf. A deaf couple.

Billy   An apprentice.

Martin   He'll show me what to do with signs. I'll learn how
to turn wood and make tables.

Billy   The two of us.

Martin   I'm going alone.
I've got it all planned. I'm just going to set off and walk.
Just head in that direction and not stop.

He points.

Billy   That's the sea.

Martin   That way then.

Billy   Bathgate. No mountains there.

Martin   Fuck off.

Billy   I'll follow you.

Martin   I'll run.

Billy   I'll chase you.

Martin   I'll kill you.

Billy   Have you told your mum and dad?

Martin   I'll leave a note.

Billy   They'll worry.

Martin   It's for the best.

Billy   They'll be hurt.

Martin   Don't try and tell me what they'll feel. You
haven't a fucking clue.

Billy   Neither have you.

Martin   I know exactly what they'll feel. I know precisely.
I can feel it for them. Better than them.
They'll feel pain.
A great amount of pain.

Billy   So stay.

Martin   I don't like them.

Billy   So. Stick it.

Martin   The longer I stay the more I want to hurt them.

Billy   Everyone gets that. That's not special.

Martin   Stay or go. Makes no difference. Either way
there'll be a great amount of pain.

Billy   Martin.
I don't want you to go without me.

Martin   You can't come.

Billy   I'll miss you.

Martin   So.

Billy   I'll feel a great amount of pain.

Martin   You attached yourself to me. If you attach yourself to someone like me you deserve pain. I have to go away and make furniture for a while. If I make furniture in a lonely place for long enough then maybe, I'll become a good person.

Billy   You believe that?

Martin   Of course I fucking don't.

Billy   Why say it then?

Martin   It's the only thing I can think of.

Billy takes **Martin**'s head in his hands, suddenly. Turns his face towards him.

Martin   Fuck off.

Billy   Look at me.

Martin   Stop it.

Billy   Look at me.

Martin is struggling but **Billy** is stronger. He holds on. **Martin** gives up struggling.

Billy   I can make you good.
Me.
You cunt.
Me.
Billy.
Understand?
I can make you good.

Billy lets go.

4

Sheena, **Paulina**, **Leo** and **Dorothy** inside the house. A model of Eden Court is on the table by **Leo**. **Sheena** is examining the model.

Sheena   This one's mine.

Leo   I realise the current fashion's against high-rise building, Mrs Mackie.

Sheena   Sheena.

Leo   Of course, Sheena. Dorothy. Will you offer Sheena some tea?

Dorothy *doesn't move.*

Sheena   Wait a minute. Is it this one? One balcony's much the same as any other, isn't it? Have you put all the windows in?

Leo   Paulina, you don't need to stay. If you don't want to. This is work.

Paulina   I'm interested.

Sheena   It could be any one of these. It depends on which way round you stand.

Paulina   I'm interested in your buildings.

Leo   Fine. Whatever.

Sheena   Something's different. The shape of it . . . colour or something . . .

Leo   It's an exact model, Mrs Mackie, an exact model of the Eden Court design. I wanted you to see this to make a point.

Sheena   The grass. You've made the grass green. Put green felt down.

Dorothy   That's the convention. All models do that.

Leo   This is the original design. Six standing towers. Aerial walkways linking each tower, platforms linking each balcony. The whole enclosing a central park . . .

Sheena   It shouldn't be green. That part of the estate's all mud now. It catches the rain. It's like a draining bowl. You want to put down brown felt for that.

Dorothy   The models aren't supposed to be realistic. They're impressions . . .

Leo   The original design was, in fact, loosely based on Stonehenge.

Paulina   I didn't think anyone lived in Stonehenge.

Leo   Standing stones were the inspiration.

Paulina   Too draughty I thought.

Sheena   Didn't you win an award for this?

Dorothy   He did.

Leo   I won some recognition at the time.

Sheena   It looks good. From this angle. From above.

Dorothy   It's about space. Architecture's about shaping space. If you look at it from here you can see how he's moulding a communal space . . .

Sheena   Were the judges in a helicopter when they gave you the award?

Leo   I was asked to build cheap homes. Cheap housing. High density accommodation . . . Eden Court is a council estate, Mrs Mackie, but I built connecting areas, and public spaces, I designed it so everyone's front room gets the sun at certain times of the day . . . They're not luxury homes, but architecturally, they're well designed. That's the point I'm making. I put as much imagination, as much thought, as much of myself into these buildings as any . . .

Dorothy   I think they're beautiful.

Leo   Objectively, aesthetically, functionally . . . Eden Court is a good estate.

Sheena   People are queueing up to leave.

Dorothy   It's a free country.

Sheena   They're unhappy. They get depressed. They get ill.
The place they live in makes them depressed.
Do you understand that?
Do you understand how important that is?

Leo   It's mass housing. You can't build mass housing to suit individual desires. It doesn't matter who designs it. You can knock it down if you want to but the problems will still be there. There'll still be unemployment, there'll still be poverty. If you want to change your circumstances Mrs Mackie.

Sheena   Sheena.

Leo   I suggest you vote labour.
I do.

Sheena   Would you say Eden Court was yours? Your building?

Leo   I designed it.

Sheena   Would you say it was your responsibility?

Leo   It was my responsibility. It's not my fault the council turned it into a ghetto. I didn't put the people in it.

Sheena   Were you there when the flats were built?

Leo   I supervised the project.

Sheena   Did you actually supervise the work? Watch every bolt go in? See every panel in place . . . ?

Leo   Of course not.

Sheena   Build them high, build them quick and build them cheap. That was the idea, wasn't it?

Leo   Not my idea.

Sheena   No, but it was the commission, wasn't it . . . what you were told?

Leo   They were designed to be built easily.

Sheena   Built in factories. Pre-cast.

Leo   It's a simple method.

Sheena   Easy to skimp on as well. Difficult to check up on mistakes.

Leo   I didn't hire the contractors.

Sheena A few bolts missing here and there. They always over-design these things anyway. If the odd panel doesn't fit, never mind.

Leo I admit there was a lack of supervision but the contractors were under pressure. Time was a pressure. You may not remember but it was you people who were demanding the houses.

Paulina That's not how I remember it.

Leo What?

Paulina I remember you talking about it. At the time. You said the job was rushed. You said it was a scandal . . .

Leo I'm not sure you know what you're talking about, Paulina.

Paulina She does.

Sheena I don't mean to seem rude, Mr Black. You're probably a nice man. You've a nice family. You probably meant for it to be a nice place to live. Isn't that what architects are for? I remember the brochures we got. A drawing of the sun shining and kids playing in the park. When they came round looking for tenants I signed like that. I saw the models. But it was all 'vision', wasn't it? Vision's the word you would use. Not houses, but a vision of housing. Everyone nicely boxed away. Cheaply accommodated. Eden Court might look like Stonehenge to you, it might have won an award but it's build like a pack of cards.

Leo It's secure. It won't fall down.

Sheena Boxes piled one on top of the other and we're stuffed in them like exhibits. You weren't asked to design houses, you were asked to house people, there's a world of difference.

Dorothy That's rubbish. It's rubbish. I've already told her she's talking rubbish, Dad.

Leo Dorothy, I think you've said enough.

Sheena   The local authority can't afford to admit the mistakes. The contractors have money. They'd probably be happy to go to court. The whole thing could take years. We don't have years. We're just ordinary people who would like decent places to live. If you give us your support they can't ignore us.

Leo   I won't lie about my own building.

Sheena   It's not your building though, is it? It never was. You just did the frippery bits that win prizes. Your stuff's just the façade. Take it away and the place is a dormitory block. Stonehenge, communal space, it doesn't mean anything if there isn't life in the place – shops, work, kids, pubs . . .

Leo   There was supposed to be . . .

Sheena   But there wasn't.

Leo   So destroy it. Blame the building. Wipe it out.

Sheena   Architecture's for the people who pay. Always. All we want to do is take control. It's not about good or bad buildings, it's about who decides. Don't we have the right to not like good buildings? You do.

Leo   I think we're agreed this is not my problem.

Sheena   But you can solve it.

Leo   I don't see why I should.

Sheena   Because it would be a good thing.

Leo   I can't help you. I'm sorry. I won't see good ideas blown up just because some people can't see beyond their own misery.

Paulina   I think you should knock them down.

Dorothy   Mum.

Paulina   If that's what people want.
At least they know what they want.
If they're sure. Then it's cruel, isn't it?

To stop them just because of history, or how things were
supposed to be. The intention.
I think you should help them.

Leo   This is about work, Paulina. This is about destroying
my work.

Sheena   I'm sorry you couldn't help us.
If you change your mind you know where to find me.

Paulina   Don't go. Why don't you stay . . . for lunch . . .
I was making lunch.

Sheen   Thank you but . . . I think I should go.
I can find my own way out.

Sheena *leaves*.

Leo   You're supposed to support me.

Paulina   I thought she was right. I thought she won the
argument.

Leo   That isn't the point. You're my wife.

Paulina *leaves*.

Leo   Well, you can forget your fucking patio.
Paulina.
You can forget your fucking patio.
Do you hear me?

Dorothy   Don't worry about it, Dad. She's mad.
Nobody's going to knock it down.
Anyone can see she's mad.

Leo   Why didn't you give me her letters?

Dorothy   They were rubbish. I told you . . .

Leo   Why didn't you give me them?

Dorothy   I told you . . . They were just . . . I didn't want
you to worry.

Leo   What's wrong with you, Dorothy?

Dorothy   Dad.

Leo   Did you think I'd made a mistake?

Dorothy   I thought . . .

Leo   I'm your father, Dorothy. I'm your employer.
How dare you humiliate me like that.
Did you think I'd built it badly?

Dorothy   No.

Leo   Did you think that was possible.

Dorothy   Please.

Leo   There was no mistake.

Dorothy   I know.

Leo   The structure is sound.

Dorothy   I know.

Leo   No mistake.

Leo *picks up the model and leaves the room. A wave of nausea passes over* **Dorothy**. **Paulina** *enters.*

Paulina   Are you sick?

Dorothy   No.

Paulina   You look like you're going to be sick.

Dorothy   I'm all right.

Paulina   Shall I bring water?

Dorothy   I'm not going to be sick.

Paulina   You're not pregnant, are you?

Dorothy   What?

Paulina   If you've got nausea.

Dorothy   I'm not pregnant.

Paulina   How do you know?

Dorothy   I know.

Paulina   Did you test yourself?

Dorothy   I know.

Paulina   Maybe you should test yourself.
You look pale.
Your complexion's . . .
There's a spot. It might be hormonal.

Dorothy   Why did you do that, Mum?

Paulina   Do what?

Dorothy   Behave like that. In front of that woman. Why?

Paulina   How did I behave?

Dorothy   As though you were neurotic. You behaved as though you were neurotic.

Paulina   I only said . . .

Dorothy   He was humiliated. In front of . . .

Paulina   I only said . . .

Dorothy   In front of everyone . . .

Paulina   I was commenting on . . .

Dorothy   You made him look small.

Paulina   What she said. The woman.

Dorothy   In front of . . .

Paulina   It made sense.

Dorothy   In front of me.
You didn't need to . . .
There was no need.

Paulina   I'm sorry. I didn't mean . . .

Dorothy   Tell him that. Say sorry to him.

Paulina approaches **Dorothy**. *Tries to touch her.*

Paulina   Dorothy.

Dorothy   Why do you have to make him . . .
Why can't you be decent to him?
You used to be decent to him.

Paulina   It's difficult . . .

Dorothy Try.

Paulina It's complicated. You wouldn't . . .

Dorothy Explain.

Paulina I really think it's best left between . . .

Dorothy Tell me.

Paulina I don't see what's to be gained from digging around in . . .

Dorothy Tell me.

Paulina In exploring this . . . landscape. Really, it's not interesting. I promise you. This situation between your father and me. It's quite . . .

Dorothy What?

Paulina Mundane.

Dorothy What?

Paulina I have no . . .
So embarrassing really.
No admiration for him.

Pause. **Dorothy** *turns away from her. Silent. Holding back tears.*

Paulina No feeling . . .

Dorothy Not good enough.

Paulina It stopped. It just finished.

Dorothy Not good enough.

Paulina I look at him now. I can't bear to . . .

Dorothy Selfish.

Paulina The way he . . .

Dorothy Selfish.

Paulina He looks so . . . failed.

Dorothy Selfish cow. You're a . . .

Paulina It's not like that.

Dorothy Selfish bloody cow.
Selfish self-centred bloody cow.

. . .

Sorry.

Paulina It can change, Dorothy. It can just . . .

Dorothy He's the same. He's the same man.
He needs you.

Paulina I know.
But it can't be like that any more.
I'm sorry.

. . .

You look pale.

Dorothy I'm fine.

Paulina You need to look after yourself.

Dorothy I'm all right.

Paulina If you worry, if you upset yourself, it shows in your skin, you know. It shows itself.

Dorothy Mum, please, just leave me alone.

Paulina You used to have such a clear complexion. Hot water. A glass of hot water. Every evening. It's cleansing. It has a cleansing effect.

Dorothy Go away, Mum. Please.

Paulina You know it's not my fault. Don't you, Dorothy?

Dorothy What does that mean?

Paulina Nothing. It means it's not my fault.

5

Darkness. The sound of a motorway. Traffic passing. **Dorothy** *is hitching. Lights pass her but no one stops.*

6

Martin *and* **Billy** *on a muddy patch of grass in Eden Court.*
Martin *is wearing the green jacket.*

Billy   This is it. This is where I'm from.

Martin   Nice.

Billy   Don't look so nervous.

Martin   I'm not nervous.

Billy   Your hands are shaking.

Billy *touches his hand.*

Martin   Piss off.

A sudden bang. It echoes. **Martin** *throws himself to the ground.*

Billy   Air-gun.

Martin   I wasn't. I just wanted to sit down.

Billy   You'll spoil your jacket. You don't know what you'll
pick up.

Martin   Seems all right to me.

Billy   Eight blocks. They're all the same. In a big circle.
You're supposed to be able to tell the time from the shadows.

Martin   Can you?

Billy   I don't know. I can only tell the time digital.
Apparently the architect committed suicide when he saw
how it turned out. It's supposed to be built backwards or
something. Probably found out it told the time backwards
and topped himself.
So what do you think?

Martin   Can't you leave?

Billy   Not unless I'm thrown out. If I got thrown out I
could be rehoused.

Martin   You could get a job.

Billy   So could you.

Martin I don't want one.

Billy Neither do I.

Martin I thought you wanted to work. I thought that was the problem. I thought you people wanted jobs.

Billy We have to say that.

Martin I thought . . .

Billy Why should I want a job? You don't. I couldn't put up with this place and a job as well. I'd die.

Martin So what d'you do all day?

Billy I'm like one of those flies. You know those flies that are born and breed and die all in one day but to the fly that day's a lifetime? That's me. Skating across the water for an afternoon.

Martin I don't know how you can stand it.

Billy I didn't say I could.

Martin I don't know how anyone could.

Billy Maybe we're a new species. Like the cockroaches.

Martin Why did you bring me here?

Billy It's where I'm from. I wanted you to see.

Martin Are you trying to make some point?

Billy No.

Martin Make me feel something.

Billy Martin, we could go somewhere. Both of us. We could both just . . . fuck off.
If we went away together.

Martin We won't.

Billy But if we did. We could even go abroad. You've got money. I could work. In a foreign country I could work. We could just get on a train now. Get on a train and fuck off to the sunshine. You and me.

Martin No.

Billy   Think about it. Greece. Spain. Italy. Amsterdam.
You and me. People think about it but nobody does it. We
could make furniture together.

Martin   Making furniture was my idea.

Billy   I could have my own idea.

Martin   You took me here to say this, didn't you?

Billy   Think about it. We could learn the language. Eat the
food. Work. Sun. Dress in Italian clothes. We could do it.

Martin   You had it all planned.

Billy   Think about it.

Martin   Make me feel bad. Make me save you.

Billy   It's not like that. It's an idea.

Martin   What do you think I am?
The White Knight of the Lavatories?
Sir Galahad of The Gents?

Billy   You need me.

Martin   In your dreams.

Billy   I like you, Martin.

Martin   So?

Billy   *Nobody else does.*

7

Dorothy *is sitting in her bedroom, in front of the mirror, in her*
underwear. **Leo** *enters without knocking.* **Dorothy** *instinctively*
covers up.

Leo   Oh. I'm sorry. Can I come in?

Dorothy   Dad.

Leo   I just thought I'd . . .

Dorothy   Do you want the seat?

Leo   I'll crouch. That's what I'll do. I'll crouch beside you. Dorothy, I . . .

He reaches out to touch her and then withdraws his hand.

I'm sorry about earlier on.

Dorothy   It's fine.

Leo   I shouldn't have shouted. I was.

Dorothy   Honestly, it's fine.

Leo   You know I love you.

Dorothy   Do you want a drink?

Leo   Sorry?

Dorothy   A lemonade? I want a lemonade. I made some. Do you want me to get you one?

Dorothy *is about to get up and go.*

Leo   Wait.
It's all right.

Dorothy   I'll get that drink, shall I?

Leo   I need to know something.
You and I . . .
We do . . . like each other, don't we?

Dorothy   I'm parched actually. (*She coughs.*)

Leo   We're friends.

Dorothy   Friends. Yes.

Leo   You're sure?

Dorothy   Course I'm sure. I think I will have that lemonade after all.

Leo   Don't go yet.

Dorothy   Whatever.

Leo   You see, Dorothy.
This is difficult for me to say.
But . . .

I feel slightly . . . alone.
At the moment.

Dorothy   Oh.

Leo   I'm telling you this because . . .
Well, because things are . . .
Martin . . . your mother. I can't seem to talk to them . . .

Dorothy   I told you. You're my dad.

Leo   I want you to know that I love you.

Dorothy   Dad, I'm sorry. I don't want to seem. It's your
business, isn't it? You and Mum. I'm glad you feel you can
talk to me. I love you. You love me. It's difficult to talk about
that sort of thing so the effort is . . . appreciated. But you
don't have to say it. That's the nice thing about families, isn't
it? You just know. You don't always have to say.

Leo   Martin isn't going to work for me, is he?
He's going to go away.

Dorothy   You don't know. He might . . .

Leo   As a father sometimes.
You think you might have made the wrong choices.
You want to ask.

Dorothy   He said he was interested.

Leo   No.

Dorothy   Time. He needs . . .

Leo   You think if you could go back . . .
I've been thinking . . .
If I could go back.
Go back to the point where the mistake happened.

Dorothy   Oh God.

Leo   What?

Dorothy   I can't.

Leo   Can't what?

Dorothy   This conversation.
Can't do it. Sorry.

Leo   I feel lost, Dorothy.
I've no plans for this.
It's not part of the design.
Tell me the truth, Dorothy . . .
Does he hate me?
Does he despise me?

Dorothy   As a matter of fact I feel very thirsty now.

She puts on her dressing-gown and leaves.

8

The sudden, loud blast of a lorry's horn. **Joe** *is in his cab driving. The radio is turned up loud. It is playing 'From Boulder to Birmingham' sung by Emmylou Harris.* **Joe** *is playing with the steering wheel.*

Joe   Pooooow Pooooow Pooooow.

9

Martin *and* **Billy** *in a gay bar. In the background a pub quiz is going on.*

Martin   Stop sulking. You took me here. I got you a drink. Fucking drink it.

Paulina *and* **Leo** *have just had sex.* **Leo** *is still in the bed.* **Paulina** *is sitting nearby.*

Leo   Do you mind if I have a cigarette?
. . .
It's been a long time.
. . .

Voice   Number Fifteen.
Pencils at the ready. Boys and Girls.
Who played the male and female leads in a. *Pretty Woman*, b. *Pretty in Pink* and c. *Pink Flamingos*?

Billy   Richard Gere, Julia Roberts . . .

Martin   You know that?

Billy   Put the answers down.

Leo *lights up a cigarette*.

Leo   I'm glad it happened. It needed to happen. I'm glad you . . .

Paulina   It was interesting.

Leo   More than interesting.

Martin *and* **Billy**.

Martin   I can't believe you know that.

Billy   Hand it in.

Paulina *and* **Leo**.

Paulina   It was an experiment. The results were interesting.

Leo   An experiment? You're my wife.

Paulina   I wish you wouldn't call me that.

Leo   Christ, not this again.

Paulina   Wife, it's so bovine. Husband. It's all so agricultural.

Billy *and* **Martin**.

Voice   Staying with pretty women . . . who had a hit with 'Oh Pretty Woman' . . . there are options in this question.

Billy   Roy Orbison.

Voice   You may prefer to wait for your options.

Billy   It's Roy Orbison.

Martin   He said you may prefer . . .

Billy   Just put it down.

Voice   Just to remind you, boys and girls, the prizes tonight are champagne, a bottle of crème de menthe and a five-pound voucher for I.G. Mellis.

Billy *has written the answer.*

Billy   Give it in.

Leo *and* **Paulina**.

Leo   Paulina.

Paulina   Have you noticed? When you can't think of anything else to say you say 'Paulina'.

Leo   Why are you spoiling this?

Paulina   You want me to be touched. Moved. As though your voice making that sound might stir me up.

Leo   Doesn't it?

Paulina   No. That's the interesting thing. Paulina. It feels like it isn't my name any more. Feels more connected with you now than with me.

Leo   What then?
What can I say to stir you up?

Paulina   Dressing-table. Bedroom. Husband. Living-room. Sofa. Carpet. Wall.

Leo   What?

Paulina   Window. Floor. Laundry basket.

Leo   Paulina.

Paulina   Dinner party. Garden. Cheeseboard. Paulina.

Leo   Are you having a breakdown? Is that what this is?

Paulina   Making love. Making love.

Leo   I thought you wanted . . . You asked me.

Paulina   You find yourself amongst these words.
You find these words being used.
You begin to notice. People say them without blinking.

Leo   You've lost me. You have to explain this.

Paulina   Everyone wants me to explain.

Leo   We go to bed in the middle of the afternoon. It's wonderful. We make up. Everything's better and then you start having some kind of breakdown. You could at least try to explain . . .

Paulina *and* **Leo**.

Paulina   I have to ask you to leave Leo.

Leo   . . .

Paulina   The house. I mean.

Leo   What the hell am I supposed to have done?

Paulina   I realise it's your house as much as it's mine. More maybe. But I'd like you to leave it. Would you do that for me? As a gesture of affection. You're not an unusually cruel man. You'd be better at living somewhere else than me.

Leo   For Christ's sake. It's not gone that far, has it?

Paulina   It will.

Leo   A trial separation.

Paulina   Not trial. A separation.

Leo   You want to throw away a marriage. Just like that.

Paulina   Not 'throw away'. Those are the wrong words.

Leo   I'm sorry. I don't have a thesaurus.

Paulina   If you could throw it away, forget it, start again etc. All those things but . . . go back to a time before it happened and follow a different route but . . . wherever I go now, for the rest of my life I'll take this marriage with me. For better or worse. I'm not throwing it away.

Leo   Why now? More than twenty years you've had, and now, today you say it's a mistake . . . why not yesterday, why not years ago?

Paulina   Fear.

Leo   Fear? Afraid of me? Don't make me laugh.

Paulina   Afraid of me. Afraid there wasn't any of me left.
Afraid I'd eroded.
. . .
I am trying, Leo . . .
Does that explain it?

Leo   No, it fucking doesn't.

Paulina   Don't you feel it? Feel yourself eroding?

Leo   No. No, I don't.

Paulina   Really?

Leo   Really.

Paulina   That's interesting.

Billy *and* **Martin**.

Billy   Wait a minute wait . . .
Ahhh . . . It's coming . . .
Rick Alessi.
Rick Alessi, Sharon Watts and Sinbad.

Martin *writes the answers down.*

Martin   How can you fill your head with this shit?
I can't believe this amount of shit can be in one head.

Billy   Just put the answer in.

Martin   Why don't we go somewhere else?

Billy   I'm winning.

Voice   Born in 1908, Indiana, Pennsylvania. No longer
alive or active in the field in which he or she first found fame.

Billy   Fuck.

Martin   I'm leaving.

Billy   Film star. Film star . . . think . . .

Martin   I said, let's go.

Leo *and* **Paulina**.

Leo   I'm sorry.

Paulina   Don't apologise.

Leo   I'm sorry.

Paulina   You haven't done anything wrong.

Leo   I didn't see.

Paulina   You're just part of a situation.

Billy *and* **Martin**.

Billy   Bette Davis!

Martin   You coming then.

Billy   Wait though, too early for Bette Davis.

Leo *and* **Paulina**.

Paulina   You're part of a situation that developed. That's all. Not your fault.

Leo   I mean more to you than that.
I think you forget sometimes, Paulina, that I know you.
I know you better than anyone.

Paulina   You know your wife. When you leave you'll notice a wife-shaped space.

Billy *and* **Martin**.

Voice   You may want to wait for your options.

Billy   Leave if you want to.

Martin   You haven't finished your drink.

Leo *and* **Paulina**.

Leo   We need to have fun again. That's all it is. We stopped having fun. Kids and everything. Responsibility. Changes you. We need to rekindle . . . get back, and . . . I can't believe you feel nothing. I can't believe there's nothing there.

Paulina   There's knowledge. I know you. Knowledge and a sort of disgust. The sort of disgust a prisoner feels for a cell mate. That's all.

Billy *and* **Martin**.

Billy Jimmy Stewart!

Martin What?

Billy *It's a Wonderful Life*!

Martin Hardly.

Billy Take it up to him. Go on.

Leo *and* **Paulina**.

Leo Does it matter that I still love you?

Paulina Sadly. No.

Leo That I need you.

Paulina Sorry.

Billy *and* **Martin**.

Billy I won the crème de menthe.
Have it.
It goes with your jacket.

Martin Can we go now?

Billy If you want.

10

Darkness. The sound of traffic passing on a motorway. **Dorothy**
hitching. No lorry stops. She clutches herself.

11

Sunset. **Leo***, holding his car keys, is standing on the balcony of an Eden
Court block.* **Sheena** *next to him.*

Sheena You can see your new site, from here.
I've watched it. Watched the cranes pull it all up.
Watched the wrecking ball.
It looks pretty from a distance. The docks and everything.
The water in the background. It's pretty.

It looks nice with the sunset.
When I first lived here I watched the ships.
Watched the men loading and unloading.
Cars and crates of whisky, loads of coal and sacks of bananas.
I thought it was a privilege. Living above the docks.
Watching over the city's front door. And then the front door
closed.
Containers.
You know the containers you put on ships, on lorries . . .
As soon as they invented containers there was no need for
docks in the city centre. No need for dockers. A port and a
motorway's all you need. The crane lifts the box out of the
ship and onto the back of the truck. Done.
So the dockers and the sailors lost their jobs and you got
yours . . . making museums and restaurants out of
warehouses and whisky bonds.
Even the tarts moved inland.
All that got left here was people who were stuck.
Stuck in boxes on the dockside waiting to be picked up.
Hoping someone's going to stop for us and take us with them.

12

The roof of a tall building. Sunset. **Billy** *and* **Martin**. **Billy** *is
drinking crème de menthe.*

Billy   Just exactly what is it that you want to do?
We wanna be free.
We wanna do what we wanna do.
And we wanna get loaded.
And we wanna have a good time.

Billy *mimes air guitar.* **Billy** *moves to touch* **Martin**. **Martin**
turns him away.

Martin   Stand still.

Billy   I want to touch you.

Martin   You can't.

Billy   I want to.

Martin   Stop talking.

A pause. **Martin** *unbuckles* **Billy**'s *belt and pulls his jeans down. Still standing behind him, he looks at* **Billy**.

Martin   Pull your shirt over your head.

Billy *does this. He is about to take the T-shirt completely off when* **Martin** *stops him.*

Martin   Leave it there. Keep your hands there. Keep your face covered.

Billy *stands still.* **Martin** *finally moves towards* **Billy** *and embraces him. Still from behind. Wanking him off.*

13

Leo *and* **Sheena** *on the balcony of Eden Court.*

Leo   Have you a family, Sheena?

Sheena   I have a son.

Leo   Grown up?

Sheena   He's dead. Same age as yours. Elliot. He was named after Elliot Gould. Does that make you laugh?

Leo   No.

Sheena   It makes me laugh. Makes me cringe to think about it.

Leo   How did he die?

Sheena   He stepped off the balcony.
I was in the kitchen. He was watching telly.
I came through and he wasn't there.
I thought he'd gone out.
They didn't know who he was when they found him.
They had to knock on all the doors in the block to see who was missing.

He was depressed. If you're depressed and there's a high balcony, apparently it's a red rag to a bull.

Leo   I'm sorry.

Sheena   Not your fault. He was depressed.

Leo   This place'd be enough to depress anybody.

Sheena   He was depressed. Elliot wasn't special. People jump here all the time. That's the trouble with architects. You think you're responsible for everything. You think it's all under your doing. You don't think this campaign's about Elliot, do you?

Leo   I don't know. Is it?

Sheena   You're not God, Mr Black. You're an architect. God's a different campaign altogether. This is about housing ... it's about people having an effect ...

Leo   A destructive effect.

Sheena   Maybe.

Leo   They've blown up others. They blew up one in Glasgow and they're blowing them up in Hackney. I don't suppose anyone'll miss this place. I don't even know if I will.

Sheena   Why did you come here, Mr Black?

Leo   To talk to you.

Sheena   What did you want to say?

Leo   I just wanted to explain ... the idea ... the dream behind this mess. It was a good ... It wasn't malicious.

Sheena   You wanted me to tell you you were a nice man.

Leo   No ...
Yes.

Sheena   It doesn't matter. Whether you're a nice man or not doesn't matter.

Leo   It does to me.

Sheena   I can't help you with that.

Leo   The new place, if they build it, it'll be exactly the same, you know.

Sheena   I'm not stupid. I'm not a silly wee woman who doesn't like modern buildings. You're right. I know this is 'good design'. 'Good design' isn't the point. The point is control. Who has the power to knock down and who has the power to build.

Leo   Even if it's wrong.

Sheena   Even if it's wrong.

14

Billy, *alone, walking along the edge of the roof, drinking crème de menthe.*

Darkness.

15

Leo, **Paulina** *and* **Dorothy** *having a meal. Silence.* **Martin** *enters.*

Martin   Any for me, Boss? I'm famished.

Leo   Sit down, Martin.

Martin   Oh. It's one of those.

Dorothy   Just sit down, will you?

Martin   The old family talk.

Leo   There's something you ought to know.

Martin   Fire away.

Leo   Your mother and I . . .

Paulina   Your father's leaving.

Martin   Oh.

Leo   Temporarily. We've decided. There's been, a tension, I'm sure you've noticed.

Martin   What do you want me to say?

Leo   This doesn't affect you, of course, this is still your home . . .

Martin   Am I supposed to say something?

Paulina   Say what you want to say.

Dorothy   Does anybody want any water?

Leo   If you want to talk about it. Of course we can talk about it.
Do you? Do you want to talk about it?

Martin   . . .
No.

Dorothy   Anyone? Water?

Leo   We'll still be a family, of course. Obviously we still . . . both of us . . . still love . . .

Martin   What about money?

Dorothy   Martin.

Martin   I'm sorry. I didn't mean to say that. I meant . . .

Leo   I don't think you need to worry about money.

Martin   Sorry.

Silence.

What are you going to do?

Paulina   What do you mean?

Martin   Now. What are you going to do. Take up singing? Hang-glide? Take a lover? Fulfil those buried dreams?

Paulina   Don't be crass.

Martin   What then?

Dorothy   If you don't mind I'll . . .

Paulina   Nothing in particular.

Dorothy   I'd like to go now. If you want me to stay I can stay . . .

Martin   Nothing in particular. All this for nothing in particular.

Dorothy   If there's anything I can do.
Is there?

Martin   Seems a bit drastic.

Dorothy   There's nothing I can do. So if you don't mind I'll go out for a while.

Paulina   You don't have to go.

Dorothy   I do.

Martin   Me too, in fact . . . said I'd be somewhere . . .

Leo   We need to talk about the future.

Martin   Who gets what?

Leo   The future, Martin . . .

Martin   Oh. I'd rather . . .
I don't know the way to speak in these situations.
Do you?
I'll only say the wrong thing again. Have the wrong idea.
I'd rather leave you to it.

Dorothy and **Martin** leave.

Leo   Martin!

Paulina   Leave them.

Leo   We can't just . . .

Paulina   Leave them.

16

The roof. **Martin** *wearing the green jacket carrying a small rucksack. An empty bottle of crème de menthe. The sound of an ambulance below.*

Martin   Billy?
Billy?
Where are you?
Billy ...
Let's go ...
We're going to Fife, Billy.
Billy?
Fuck.

Darkness.

17

Leo *with the model of Eden Court.* **Paulina** *near him.*

Leo   In the past we built cities on top of cities ...
in the middle of cities ...
around them ...
Haphazard, unplanned ... encrustations.
Layers of mistakes corrected by more mistakes ...
Never a clean slate.
Never a clear vision.
So when they asked me to build something I thought ...
Duty required me to ...
I thought I had to make ...
Because of the future ...
A new idea. A better thing.
Look.
A thousand families ... self-contained flats ... connecting
walkways ... public galleries and ... space and ...
structure and ...
And the stones ... each block represents a stone, a
monolith ...
Do you see? Timeless.
A family in each flat.
Each block a community.
The whole estate a village.
The city encircled by estates, each one connected to the
others and to the centre.

Everything connected to the centre.
Do you see?
A design.
But it's the human element, isn't it?
Materials structure and so on . . . but the human
element . . .
Eludes you.
You can't design for it.

Paulina   Maybe they'll ask you to build the new ones.

Leo   I don't think so.

Paulina   Maybe you and Martin.
It could be a project for you.

Leo   Maybe.

Paulina   You could offer. Put in a plan . . .

Leo   No point in a plan.

Paulina   Why not?

Leo   No point in planning if anything you build can be
turned into a prison.

Paulina   Houses though, Leo.

Leo   Anything you think up can be made dangerous.

Paulina   Still. You and Martin. You could teach him. Talk
to him. Make progress.

Leo   No matter how high you build something. No matter
how well you build it. No matter how beautiful it is. You
can't build a thing high enough that if you fell off you
wouldn't hit the ground.

18

A morgue. **Martin** *sitting next to* **Billy**'s *body*. **Dorothy** *comes in.*

Dorothy   Who is he?

Martin   A friend. An acquaintance. He had my name in his pocket. That's all.

Dorothy   When you phoned . . . you sounded like you wanted someone.

Martin   Did I? I've been trying all my life to sound like that. Never managed before.

Dorothy   Is he a . . . did you . . . ?

Martin   We fucked a few times.

Dorothy   I'm sorry.

Martin   He ran off the roof of a block of flats.
Spoiled his looks apart from anything else.
His body sort of burst. He spoiled himself.
You don't get the right impression seeing him like this.

Dorothy   Do you know why he did it?

Martin   I was going to leave and he wanted to come with me. I wouldn't let him.

Dorothy   It's not your fault, Martin.

Martin   I know.

Dorothy   You mustn't feel it's your fault.

Martin   I don't.

Dorothy   Do his family know yet?

Martin   No.

Dorothy   Will you tell them?

Martin   I don't know who they are. Don't even know if he's got one. I never asked. Someone else'll tell them. There must be someone who's job it is to tell people that kind of thing.

Dorothy *goes over to hold* **Martin**.

Martin   Don't. It makes me feel uncomfortable.

Dorothy   Sorry.

Martin *touches* **Billy**'s *face. Gingerly.*

Dorothy   Do you want me to leave?

Martin   No. Stay.

Dorothy   I don't know what to say.

Martin   What effect do you want?

Dorothy   Sorry?

Martin   You want to say the right thing. What effect would saying the right thing achieve?

Dorothy   I want to comfort you.

Martin   Don't say anything then. I'll try and feel that anyway. Save you searching for words.

Dorothy   He was young.

Martin   I've never seen a dead body before. I've dreamt of it. I've thought about what it would be like. I've imagined myself dead. Everyone crowded round me. Tears etc. I've imagined you dead. Never seen it though. It's not as dramatic as I thought. It's not as beautiful. It's just Billy's empty.

Dorothy   Maybe he's in a better place. Happy somewhere.

Martin   What an ugly thought.

Dorothy   I only meant ... we don't know.

Martin   The interesting thing is. Looking at him. Now. Me beside him. You here watching. I feel. Quite happy in a way. I feel powerful. It's almost erotic. As though for the first time I'm entitled to be ... anything. I'm entitled to say ... anything. To do anything. I could make a pass at you, or spit at you, or weep and you wouldn't ask me to explain, I'd be entitled.

Dorothy   Maybe.

Martin   What do you fucking mean maybe. Of course I fucking could. You'd do anything for me. You fucking worship me. You came here, didn't you? I told you to and you came, didn't you?

Dorothy Yes.

Martin See.
You've got that look on your face.
Tolerance.
Awe.
Fear.
When I came to the reception the woman looked at me.
She gave me that look.
I want everyone to look at me that way.
Always.
Maybe I'll have to kill you next.

Dorothy We should leave. We're not his real family. We shouldn't be here.

Martin You go. I want to stay.

Dorothy Will you be long?

Martin I don't think I ever want to move.

Dorothy *leaves.* **Martin** *looks at* **Billy** *for a while. He kisses* **Billy**. *Holds him.*

Martin Fuck. Fuck. Fuck. Fuck.

Darkness.

19

Leo *and* **Sheena**, *in* **Leo**'s *office, studying blueprints.*

Sheena I came to say thank you.

Leo No need.

Sheena I wanted to.

Leo Where have they moved you to?

Sheena Temporary places. Near the motorway.

Leo Very nice.

Sheena   I've been working on the new designs.
It's a woman, the person we're working with.
You maybe know her. She does community architecture.

Leo   Probably not.

Sheena   She's very good. Helpful . . .

Leo   I'm glad.

Sheena   What are you doing?

Leo   The demolition people need blueprints so the
explosives can be placed correctly. At the points of weakness.
They need to know where the weaknesses are so they can
design the explosion. They want the structure to fall in on
itself.

Sheena   And you know where the weaknesses are?

Leo   I thought so.

Sheena   I just thought you'd put a bomb under it.

Leo   It's a complex job destroying buildings as big as this.
You can't just watch it topple. It's more clinical than that,
more surgical. The taller the building the more you need to
control it, or else the whole thing falls sideways, takes other
buildings with it, falls into the crowd. It's an interesting
operation.

Sheena   Will you be there? On the day?

Leo   Maybe.

Sheena   There'll be quite a crowd.

Leo   People love to watch things fall. The bigger the better.

Sheena   One of the kids from the estate won the
competition to press the detonator.

Leo   It's not a real detonator, you know.

Sheena   Really?

Leo   Just for show. Engineers control the process. It's all
computerised nowadays. The kid's just there for the
cameras.

Sheena   I hope nobody tells him. It'd be like telling him Santa Claus doesn't exist.

Leo   Do you still have a set of keys, Ms Mackie?

Sheena   Keys?

Leo   For your flat.

Sheena   I think so. Why?

Leo   I'd like to borrow them.

Sheena   What for?

Leo   Last look around. Take some photos. Nostalgia. Keep a record of them before they go.

Sheena   If you want. I don't need them.

She gives him a set of keys.

Leo   Thank you.

Sheena   You know, I fancy this job, Mr Black.
Do you think you can do courses?
At my age?

Leo   I'm sure you can.

Sheena   Now the campaign's finished I'm fired up for something new ... You know. I feel ... Do you think I'd be any good?

Leo   You've got strong ideas.

Sheena   I'd really like to do it.

Leo   You should.

Sheena   Maybe I could work for you.

Leo   I'd be happy to have you.

Sheena   That's nice of you to say.

Leo   I mean it.

Sheena   Well. I came to say thank you for what you've done.

Leo   Don't mention it.

Sheena   I know my way out.

Leo   Good luck. Ms Mackie.

20

Dorothy *and* **Joe** *in the cab of* **Joe***'s lorry.*

Dorothy   Where are we going this time?

Joe   Glasgow.

Dorothy   What's Glasgow like?

Joe   Violent.

Dorothy   I thought Glaswegians were supposed to be friendly.

Joe   Violent but friendly. That's supposed to be the characteristic.

Dorothy   Maybe I should stay there.

Joe   Running away again?

Dorothy   I missed you. I waited for you at the side of the road but you never stopped.

Joe   I must have missed you too. Didn't see you or something. I had my eyes straight ahead. I don't often look for hitchers, you get hypnotised by the road.

Dorothy   I tried sending you dolphin calls. You mustn't have picked them up.

Joe   Maybe I did. I stopped this time.

Dorothy   What's in the back?

Joe   Who knows? It's a container. I pick up the box from the boat. Could be anything. Machinery. Grain. Meat. Metal. Anything. Could be empty.

Dorothy   You're a nice man, Joe.

Joe   Don't say that.

Dorothy   Why not? You are.

Joe   You don't know anything about me.

Dorothy   I don't need to. I can tell.

Joe   I could be a killer. Or a rapist. Maybe I pick up women and rape them in the back of the truck. Other drivers do.

Dorothy   Do you?

Joe   No.

Dorothy   Have you thought about it?

Joe   Yes.

Dorothy   You wouldn't.

Joe   That's what I say.

Dorothy   Did you miss me?

Joe   A little.

Dorothy   Do you love me?

Joe   No.

Dorothy   Could you love me?

Joe   I'll take you anywhere you want to go. I'll do anything you want me to do. I'll talk to you all night. That's better than love. You don't want me to love you.

Dorothy   How do you know?

Joe   If I loved you I'd hurt you.

Dorothy   You're a nice man, Joe.

21

The sound of dripping water. A gents' public toilet. **Martin** *stands in a urinal, a Jenners' bag next to him.*

22

Dorothy *and* **Joe** *in the truck.*

23

Paulina *potting plants.*

24

Leo *opens the door to an empty flat.*

A siren.

A voice speaks through a loud hailer.

Voice   STAND CLEAR!
STAND CLEAR!
STAND CLEAR PLEASE.
STAND WELL BACK.

The siren sounds a second time.

Leo *is alone. He looks out of the window. The sound of a crowd
chanting 'ten, nine, eight, seven, six, five, four, three, two, one . . .'
There is a moment of stillness.*

Darkness.

The sound of a series of explosions.

The sound of a crowd cheering and clapping.

Methuen Modern Plays

include work by

Jean Anouilh
John Arden
Margaretta D'Arcy
Peter Barnes
Sebastian Barry
Brendan Behan
Edward Bond
Bertolt Brecht
Howard Brenton
Simon Burke
Jim Cartwright
Caryl Churchill
Noël Coward
Sarah Daniels
Nick Dear
Shelagh Delaney
David Edgar
Dario Fo
Michael Frayn
John Godber
Paul Godfrey
John Guare
Peter Handke
Jonathan Harvey
Iain Heggie
Declan Hughes
Terry Johnson
Barrie Keeffe
Stephen Lowe
Doug Lucie

John McGrath
David Mamet
Patrick Marber
Arthur Miller
Mtwa, Ngema & Simon
Tom Murphy
Phyllis Nagy
Peter Nichols
Joseph O'Connor
Joe Orton
Louise Page
Joe Penhall
Luigi Pirandello
Stephen Poliakoff
Franca Rame
Philip Ridley
Reginald Rose
David Rudkin
Willy Russell
Jean-Paul Sartre
Sam Shepard
Wole Soyinka
C. P. Taylor
Theatre de Complicite
Theatre Workshop
Sue Townsend
Judy Upton
Timberlake Wertenbaker
Victoria Wood

Methuen World Classics *and*
Methuen Contemporary Dramatists

Aeschylus (two volumes)
Jean Anouilh
John Arden (two volumes)
Arden & D'Arcy
Aristophanes (two volumes)
Aristophanes & Menander
Peter Barnes (three volumes)
Brendan Behan
Aphra Behn
Edward Bond (four volumes)
Bertolt Brecht
    (five volumes)
Howard Brenton
    (two volumes)
Büchner
Bulgakov
Calderón
Jim Cartwright
Anton Chekhov
Caryl Churchill
    (two volumes)
Noël Coward (five volumes)
Sarah Daniels (two volumes)
Eduardo De Filippo
David Edgar (three volumes)
Euripides (three volumes)
Dario Fo (two volumes)
Michael Frayn (two volumes)
Max Frisch
Gorky
Harley Granville Barker
    (two volumes)
Henrik Ibsen (six volumes)
Terry Johnson

Lorca (three volumes)
David Mamet (three volumes)
Marivaux
Mustapha Matura
David Mercer (two volumes)
Arthur Miller
    (five volumes)
Anthony Minghella
Molière
Tom Murphy
    (three volumes)
Musset
Peter Nichols (two volumes)
Clifford Odets
Joe Orton
Louise Page
A. W. Pinero
Luigi Pirandello
Stephen Poliakoff
    (two volumes)
Terence Rattigan
Willy Russell
Ntozake Shange
Sam Shepard (two volumes)
Sophocles (two volumes)
Wole Soyinka
David Storey (two volumes)
August Strindberg
    (three volumes)
J. M. Synge
Sue Townsend
Ramón del Valle-Inclán
Frank Wedekind
Oscar Wilde

New titles also available from Methuen

Klaus Chatten & Sergi Belbel
Sugar Dollies & After the Rain
0 413 70790 3

John Godber
Lucky Sods & Passion Killers
0 413 70170 0

Paul Godfrey
A Bucket of Eels & The Modern Husband
0 413 68830 5

Jonathan Harvey
Boom Bang-A-Bang & Rupert Street Lonely Hearts Club
0 413 70450 5

Stig Larsson & Nikolai Kolyada
Sisters, Brothers & The Oginski Polonaise
0 413 70780 6

Gregory Motton & Elfriede Jelinek
Cat and Mouse (Sheep) & Services
0 413 70760 1

Phyllis Nagy
Weldon Rising & Disappeared
0 413 70150 6

Judy Upton
Bruises & The Shorewatchers' House
0 413 70430 0

For a Complete Catalogue of Methuen Drama titles
write to:

Methuen Drama
Michelin House
81 Fulham Road
London SW3 6RB

A Methuen Fast Track Playscript

First published in Great Britain in 1996
by Methuen Drama
an imprint of Reed International Books Ltd
Michelin House, 81 Fulham Road, London SW3 6RB
and Auckland, Melbourne, Singapore and Toronto
in association with the Traverse Theatre
Cambridge Street, Edinburgh EH1 2ED
and distributed in the United States of America
by Heinemann, a division of Reed Elsevier Inc.
361 Hanover Street, Portsmouth, New Hampshire
NH 03801 3959

Revised and reprinted 1996

ISBN 0 413 70770 9

A CIP catalogue record for this book is available from the British
Library

Typeset by Wilmaset Ltd, Birkenhead, Wirral
Printed in Great Britain by Cox & Wyman Ltd, Reading,
Berkshire

THE ARCHITECT

David Greig

**Published by Methuen Drama in association
with the Traverse Theatre**